First published Sheffield 2012

© Lou Radford:

Lou Radford asserts the moral right to be identified as the author of this work

This study is presented as a collection of historical information about the use of herbs in the past. The text also covers the modern uses of herbs, including information relating to the various theories and practices underlying the use of herbs as natural remedies. This study does not represent an endorsement or guarantee as to the efficacy of any remedy, or its preparation. The remedies are not intended to replace or supersede medical consultation and treatment.

Acknowledgements

I would like to thank my dear Grand-dad (Wilfred Goodman) for first introducing me to herbal medicine, he did not have a large pharmacopeia (just two herbs actually) but his complete faith in their medicinal value was enough to start me on the journey that has led me here. I can still recall the bitter taste of the Roman chamomile he gave me whilst I was recovering from my endless bilious attacks and the intense scent of the elderflowers drying in his potting shed. I miss him.

Thanks are also due to the other members of my long-suffering family who have supported me throughout. I would also like to give special thanks to my dear friends Julie Bowman an exceptional light weaver and Rafe Nauen the brother I never thought I would have this lifetime.

The mistakes are all my own!

Lou Radford

Table of Contents

Acknowledgements 3

Glossary of terms used 6

Materia Medica 8

    Balm: *Melissa Officinalis* 9

    Blackberry: *Rubus Fruticosus* 11

    Burdock: *Arctium Lappa* 13

    Cayenne: *Capsicum Minimum* 15

    Chickweed: *Stellaria Media* 17

    Clover (Red): *Trifolium Pratense* 19

    Coltsfoot: *Tussilago Farfara* 21

    Comfrey: *Symphytum Officinale* 23

    Dandelion: *Taraxacum Officinale* 25

    Echinacea: *Echinacea Angustifolia* 27

    Elder: *Sambucus Nigra* 29

    Garlic: *Allium Sativum* 32

    Ginger: *Zingiber Officinale* 35

    Hawthorn: *Crataegus Oxyacantha* 37

    Lavender: *Lavendula Augustafolia(formerly Lavendula Officinalis)* 40

    Marigold: *Calendula Officinalis* 42

    Meadowsweet: *Spiraea Ulmaria* 45

    Mugwort: *Artemisia Vulgaris* 47

    Nettle: *Urtica Dioica* 49

    Peppermint: *Mentha Piperita* 51

    Plantain: *plantago Major* 53

    Raspberry: *Rubus Idaeus* 55

    Rose Hips: *Rosa Canina* 57

    Sage: *Salvia Officinallis* 59

    St John's Wort: *Hypericum Perforatum* 62

    Wormwood: *Artemisia Absinthum* 64

    Yarrow: *Achillea Millefolium* 66

The How To Section 68

Section one: Gathering and drying plant materials 69

    Gathering herbs 69

    Drying plant materials 70

    Storing dried plant materials 71

Section two: Water based herbal preparations 72

    Herbal infusions 72

    Herbal Decoctions 73

Section Three: Alcohol based herbal preparations 74
Tinctures 74

Section Four: External Applications 75
Baths 75
Compress 75
Poultices 75
Liniments 76
Infused Oils 76
Creams and ointments 78
Lotions 79

The Recipes 85
Balm 82
Blackberry 85
Burdock 89
Cayenne 91
Chickweed 94
Clover 96
Coltsfoot 97
Dandelion 98
Elder 99
Elderberries 101
Garlic 103
Ginger 106
Hawthorn 108
Lavender 109
Marigold (calendula) 110
Meadowsweet 113
Nettles 115
Sage 119
Wormwood 120

Appendices 121

Appendix i 122
The actions of some readily available herbs 122

Appendix ii 124
Repertory: (specifically herbs from this volume) 124

Bibliography 127

Glossary of terms used

Here are some terms that you may not be familiar with that are used in this book.

Alterative: Gradually restoring healthy bodily functions

Anti-Microbial: These herbs help rid the body of pathogenic micro-organisms

Anti-spasmodic: Use these herbs to alleviate cramps or spasms

Anti-tusive: Capable of relieving or suppressing coughing

Aromatic: These herbs will help to stimulate the digestive system. Also useful to add flavour to other, less palatable, medicines

Astringent: An astringent herb contains tannins these agents contract tissue and thus help to reduce secretions and discharges. Astringents will reduce the swelling in haemorrhoids and relieve swollen tonsils.

Bitter: The bitter taste of these herbs can help stimulate the digestive system.

Cardiac tonic: These tonics affect the heart

Carminative: herbs rich in volatile oils that relax the stomach, support digestion and relieve bloating and wind.

Cholagogue: All bitter herbs are cholagogue to some degree. These herbs increase the flow of bile

Demulcent: These herbs can help to soothe and protect irritated or inflamed internal tissue.

Depurative: These herbs help cleanse waste products and toxins from the body. Depurative herbs work by supporting the natural cleansing functions of the kidneys liver and large intestines they also increase tissue blood flow and lymph drainage.

Diaphoretic: Use these herbs to aid elimination of toxins through the skin. Diaphoretics will increase perspiration.

Diuretic: To increase the flow and elimination of urine

Emmenagogue: Use Emmenagogue herbs to normalise and stimulate menstruation.

Emollient: These herbs will shield, soften and soothe when applied to the skin.

Expectorant: The expectorants help the body to expel surplus mucus from the respiratory tract

Febrifuge: Used to reduce fevers

Hepatic: The hepatic herbs aid the liver by toning it and increasing the flow of bile

Hypotensive: These herbs help the body regulate and normalize elevated blood pressure.

Laxative: Use laxatives to gently relieve constipation

Nervine: These herbs can help strengthen and tone the nervous system. Some act as stimulants and some as relaxants.

Pectoral: Pectorals strengthen and heal the respiratory system.

Rubefacient: A rubefacient will stimulate the dilation of the capillaries causing the blood to flow from deeper in the body and this action will often relieve internal pains.
Sedative: Sedatives calm the nervous system and reduce stress
Sialagogue: Herbs with a sialagogue action stimulate the flow of saliva from the salivary glands
Soporific: These herbs will help induce restful sleep
Stimulant: Stimulants give the body a boost of energy
Styptic: The styptic herbs will reduce or external bleeding by their astringency.
Tonic: Tonics strengthen and enliven the body either in part or as a whole
Vulnerary: These herbs are applied externally to aid the body in the healing of wounds.

Materia Medica
(The Herbs)

Balm: *Melissa Officinalis*
Garden herb: Easy to grow

Parts used: leaves
Gathering: the leaves can be harvested two or three times a year usually between June and September. Cut off the young shoots when they are about a foot long.
Actions:
Carminative
Anti-spasmodic
Anti-depressive
Diaphoretic
Hypotensive
Indications: Balm is a specific remedy for indigestion and flatulence because it serves to relieve spasms in the digestive tract thereby easing cramping. Its anti-depressive action means that balm is particularly recommended when digestive problems are associated with stress of any kind. Balm lifts the spirit, sharpens the senses and heightens comprehension. It also has a tonic effect on the circulatory system and the heart and can help to lower blood pressure. Balm is an effective diaphoretic and can be taken to lower the temperature when fever is present.

Preparation and dosage:
Infusion: 2-3 tsp of dried herb or fresh leaves to taste. The tea should be covered to prevent the volatile oils from escaping, brew for 10-15 minutes. Take a cup three times a day.
Tincture: take 2-6mls of the tincture three times a day.
Folklore, History and Kitchen Witch: Balm is one of the herbs attributed to Jupiter and such herbs generally have a relaxing, calming and soothing disposition. These very attributes were noted by John Gerard in 1597 when he informed us that: 'bewme drunk in wine comforteth the hart (sic), and driveth away all melancholie and sadness'.

Over time, balm has taken on an almost legendary reputation for encouraging good health and longevity. It was highly esteemed by the 16th century botanist and alchemist Paracelsus as the *'Primum ens Melisso'* (a kind of tincture whose main ingredient was balm) that he believed would completely revivify a man. Later, 1n 1696, the London dispensary declared that "An essence of balm given in Canary wine every morning will renew youth, strengthen the brain, relieve languishing nature, and prevent baldness". More recently still in the 1930's in the very reliable

<u>Modern Herbal</u> Mrs Grieve reports the story of John Hussey of Sydenham, who lived to the age of 116. Grieve clearly implies that Hussey reached this age because he 'breakfasted for fifty years on balm tea sweetened with honey'. These claims for the wonders of balm tea may or may not be accurate but I for one can think of no nicer way to start the day.

In the past it was widely known that balm had a positive effect on bees, in fact its name, Melissa, is Greek for honeybee. Gerard noted that: 'it (balm) is profitably planed where bees are kept. The hives of bees being rubbed with the leaves of bawme, causeth the bees to keep together, causeth others to come with them and when they have strayed away they do find their way home by it.'

Actually, having balm in the garden seems to be an all round good idea as according to a number of authorities, including the American herbalist and essence maker, Judy Griffin, balm is an excellent companion plant for tomatoes, parsley, fennel and onions.

Balm can also be used externally to good effect, as its scent is very calming to the mind. Balm makes a wonderfully soothing bath additive, which according to Catherine Palmer was popular enough in the past to have mention in some 14th century monastic annals. It is reported in the abbey archives of Ste Yuste that when Charles V of France (1338 – 1380) stayed in the monastery he used an infusion of balm in his bathwater because he claimed that bathing in this herb sharpened his wits. Here is yet another nod to balm's strong connection with the workings of the brain.

In the 17th century, being aware of the beautiful scent of balm, the Carmelite nuns of Paris distilled the leaves to make Carmelite water – I have included a recipe for this very popular perfume which was the forerunner of eau-de-cologne in the recipe section.

Balm is included in my recipe for a herb pillow to encourage peaceful sleep. The pillow should be filled with a mixture of the dried flowers of hops, cowslips and balm.

A simple charm to make the wearer loved by all is made by enclosing a small amount of dried lemon balm in a little cloth bag, which is then worn about the person.

Blackberry: *Rubus Fruticosus*
Hedgerow herb: common

Parts used: leaves, root and berries
Gathering: Collect leaves and roots between May and September. The bramble fruits from August to November, however berries should be collected before the first frost
Actions:
Anti-oxidant
Astringent
Tonic
Mildly analgesic
The berries are a good source of both citric (vitamin C) and malic acid[1].
Indications: Blackberries have a tonic effect and will help sustain general good health. Blackberry leaf tea is an astringent and has been used as a treatment for diarrhoea and dysentery. Blackberry syrup or jelly (see recipe section) are both soothing for sore throats when taken neat on a spoon.

Preparation and dosage:
Infusion: 1 teaspoon of dried or 1 tablespoon of fresh herb to each cupful of water. Brew for 10-15 minutes. Drink a cupful hourly for the first four hours and then three times a day if needed.

For a warming winter drink mix blackberry vinegar or syrup as desired with hot water to boost Vitamin C levels and cheer the spirit in the winter months.

Folklore, History and Kitchen Witch: Blackberries fall under the dominion of Venus. Lilly, in his Christian Astrology informs us that this means they have a sweet flavour, a pleasant smell, a white flower and their leaves are smooth and not jagged. The horrible barbs of the bramble seem to be in conflict with the idea of a Venusian plant which one would imagine to be gentle however, Lilly's contemporary, Nicholas Culpepper, clears this up, by saying that although brambles are a herb of Venus they in Aries the house of Mars... and hence they have nasty thorns.

---

[1] Malic Acid: useful for boosting immunity, maintaining oral health, reducing the risk of poisoning from a build-up of toxic metals and promoting smoother and firmer skin.

Bramble roots have been use as medicine for long ages they are mentioned in a 10th century translation of a leech book, which is believed to be of early Anglo-Saxon origin. You will note the author as made the addition of several Christian incantations to this prescription. The Bramble's astringent properties are noted, it says:

'Against dysentery, a bramble of which both ends are in the earth take the newer root, delve it up, cut up nine chips with the left hand and sing three times the *miserere mei deus* and nine times the *pater noster*, then take mugwort and everlasting, boil these three worts and the chips in milk till they get red, then let the man sip at night fasting a pound dish full ... let him rest himself soft and wrap himself up warm; if more need be let him do so again, if thou still need do it a third time, thou wilt not need oftener.'

You will notice the repetition of the numbers nine and three in this early prescription and there is a reason for this. The early Anglo-Saxons believed that 'flying venoms' caused disease. Their folklore ran: When the God Woden smote the serpent with nine magic twigs, the serpent was broken into nine parts, from which the wind blew the nine flying venoms. Consequently, the number nine became very important in healing and there are numerous instances of patients being directed to take nine of each of the ingredients or to take the herb potion itself for nine days. Sometimes, an incantation has to be said or sung three or nine times.[2]

The 16th century herbalist John Gerard notes that blackberries are good for soreness of the mouth and throat.[3]

Culpepper recommends the bramble for: 'ulcers and putrid sores of the mouth and throat, and for the quinsy' and says that they 'likewise heal other fresh wounds and sores'.

There is traditionally a date after which the berries should not be picked, most commonly taken to be Michaelmas (29 September), after which time the devil is said to spit or stamp (or worse) on the berries.

---

[2] These incantations were usually Christian because the only surviving leech books were committed to vellum after the arrival of Christianity to the south of England in 579

[3] It has since been found that blackberries contain a mild analgesic in the form of salicylic acid (from Latin salix, willow tree, from the bark of which the substance used to be obtained)

Burdock: *Arctium Lappa*

Hedgerow herb: common

Parts used: Roots and rhizome

Gathering: The roots and rhizome should be unearthed in September or October the root are deep and you will need a good spade and a hand trowel to get them out

Actions:
Alterative
Bitter
Depurative
Diuretic
Diaphoretic

Indications: Burdock is widely acknowledged as one of the best blood purifiers available. It is always one of the first herbs to try with all skin disorders particularly if the skin is dry and scaly. Taken internally it is especially useful for eczema and psoriasis where it can be combined with red clover and yellow dock to good effect. This treatment can be accompanied by the application of compresses or poultices to any outward skin eruptions. A decoction of the root is very useful for boils and rheumatic complaints.

Burdock will aid digestion and stimulate appetite, it should, therefore, be considered for any eating disorder including anorexia nervosa. This herb will also aid kidney function and can be very effective in the treatment of cystitis. Especially when combination with dandelion and echinacea burdock is a very useful remedy for any kidney complaints where a diuretic and anti-microbial effect is needed. Burdock can be used externally as a compress or poultice to facilitate the healing of wounds or sores.

Preparation and dosage: Decoction: place I teaspoon of dried or 2 teaspoons of fresh root to each cup of water in a saucepan. Boil for 10-15 minutes with a lid on. Sweeten and cool. Take a cupful three times a day

For external use on compress or poultice or as a bath additive

Tincture: take 2-4 ml three times a day

Folklore, History and Kitchen Witch: Burdock is under the rule of Venus and therefore this herb is a potent charm. A root of burdock in a medicine pouch will help the keeper of the pouch to find spiritual nourishment and bring deep healing.

It has been shown that burdock was part of the pharmacy of Hippocrates which means that its medicinal use pre-dates 460 BC. The Roman botanist, Piny the Elder mentions five remedies that can be made with burdock in his <u>Natural History</u> and this confirms its continuing use in Roman times.

In the Anglo-Saxon <u>Leech Book II</u> burdock is part of a remedy for baldness and indeed its reputation as a hair tonic remains to this day. I have included a recipe for a simple hair tonic to add shine to dull hair in the recipe section.

In 1578 Henry Lyte informs us in his <u>Niewe herbal</u> that: 'the leaves pound with a little salt is with great profit laid unto the bitings and stingings of serpents, madde dogs and other venomous beasts' and in his 1597 <u>Herbal</u> Gerard writes extensively about burdock and refers a great deal to the Greek Physician Dioscoides, whose work he had plainly read and copied.

In the 17th century Nicholas Culpepper seems as enamored as his forebears with burdock in his <u>Complete Herbal</u> (1649) he repeats the claims of Lyte and Gerard and also adds that the external application of burdock to various parts of the body would move the uterus and stay the child within it.

Mrs. Grieve reports that the name of the genus, *arctium*, is derived from the Greek *arktos*, a bear she thinks perhaps alluding to the roughness of the burrs. *Lappa*, the specific name, is derived from a word meaning to seize. Or as Shakespeare put it in measure for measure 'Nay, friar, I am a kind of Burr, I shall stick'.

Cayenne: *Capsicum Minimum*

Garden herb

Parts used: The Fruit

Gathering: The pods should be gathered when they are fully ripe and dried in the shade.

Actions:

Antiseptic

Carminative

Rubefacient

Sialagogue

Stimulant

Tonic

Indications: Cayenne is a fantastic systemic stimulant. Its tonic effect is a specific for the circulatory system and as such it will regulate the blood flow. Cayenne will thus help to balance and fortify the action of the heart, arteries, capillaries and nerves. The master herbalist Richard Schulze reports that: "Cayenne should be a herb which everyone has in the kitchen, the bathroom and in the trunk of their car...because there is no other herb that moves the blood faster to the brain than cayenne. ...It relieves the pain of angina pectoris by helping to get more blood to the heart muscle itself. And if a person has a heart attack, Cayenne is the surest first-aid remedy...I have had almost a hundred patients actually save their lives by using a tablespoon of Cayenne pepper in a glass of warm water and drinking it down fast."

Cayenne has been shown to lower cholesterol and remove toxins from the bloodstream. It is effective in the treatment of cold hands and feet where peripheral blood flow is poor. Cayenne is also taken internally to shrink haemorrhoids.

When combined with tincture of myrrh it can be used as a gargle for laryngitis or as a general antiseptic wash on unbroken skin.

Externally cayenne is an excellent rubefacient when added to a liniment for the treatment of rheumatic pains, lumbago and numbness of the limbs.

Preparation and dosage: Infusion: to ½ to 1 teaspoonful of cayenne add a cup of boiling water and leave to infuse for 10-15 minutes. Mix a tablespoon of this mixture with hot water and drink as required.

Tincture: take between ¼ and 1 ml of the tincture three times a day or when required

<u>Folklore, History and Kitchen Witch</u>: Cayenne falls under the dominion of Mars because of its bright red colour and its hot spicy nature. Actually, its name is derived from the Greek 'to bite'.

According to a study at Hamilton University, to date, the oldest known records of peppers come from the desert valley of Tehuanacán, 150 miles south of Mexico City. Studies of seeds and fossilised human dung found in ancient cave dwellings show that the indigenes were eating peppers as early as 7,000 B.C. It is assumed that the first peppers consumed were picked from wild plants. It is thought that Peppers were one of the first plants to be domesticated in the Americas and it can be said with some confidence that they were first grown domestically between 5,000 and 3,000 B.C.

David Wolfe in his homage to cacao <u>Naked Chocolate</u> claims that Cayenne was a vital ingredient of the ritual Mayan chocolate drink because it intensified the efficacy of the brew by dilating the capillaries thus allowing the sacred cacao potion to reach the cells more easily.

The first westerners to document its medicinal uses were explorers accompanying Columbus on his voyages. Cayenne makes a brief appearance in Gerard's <u>Herbal</u> of 1597 where it is called Ginne or Indian pepper. Gerard says ' it warmeth the stomacke, and helpeth greatly the digestion of meates'.

Culpepper seems terrified of the taste, feel and smell of cayenne it is almost risible to read his account. He says 'they burn and inflame the throat so extremely that it is hard to be endured, and if it be outwardly applied to the skin on any part of the body it will exulcerate and raise it as if it had been burnt with fire or scalded with hot water. The vapours that arise from the husks will pierce the brain, by flying up into the head through the nostrils as to procure violent sneezings, and draw down abundance of thin rheum, forcing tears from the eyes, and will all pass into the throat, and provoke sharp coughing, and cause violent vomiting' I think we can deduce that Culpepper was not a fan of spicy foreign foods.

In the 1920's Kloss claimed the spice to be a veritable natural wonder drug and dedicated more pages to cayenne in his ground breaking <u>Back to Eden</u> than any other single herb.

Chickweed: *Stellaria Media*
Hedgerow herb: common

Parts Used: Dried aerial parts

Gathering: Chickweed is usually at its best between May and July but can be collected at any time of year. Gather using scissors rather than pulling it up by the roots (or it gets covered in soil which you then have to clean off)

Actions:
Anti-rheumatic
Demulcent
Emollient
Vulnerary

Indications: Chickweed is used to make a soothing healing ointment that is particularly useful for itching and irritation of the skin this means that this ointment is particularly useful for the external treatment of eczema and psoriasis. Chickweed, either as a compress or as ointment, is recommended for the healing of cuts and grazes, inflamed insect bites and haemorrhoids.

A poultice of Chickweed enclosed in muslin is excellent for inflammation and external ulcers and a sure remedy for a carbuncle or an external abscess. The water in which the plant material is boiled should also be used to bathe the affected part.

Internally Chickweed is used for the treatment of rheumatism.

Chickweed tea is effective when taken for constipation and useful to ease coughs and hoarseness.

Preparation and dosage: Infusion 2 teaspoons of dried or 4 teaspoons of fresh herb to a cup of water, steep for five minutes. Drink a cupful three times a day.

Externally chickweed is made into an ointment or can be used as a poultice (see how to section).

There is no finer cure for irritated itchy skin than a strong infusion of chickweed (about a handful of fresh plant material) added to bathwater.

Folklore, History and Kitchen Witch: Chickweed is under the rule of the Moon as it is a cooling, succulent plant full of water.

According to the archaeological record chickweed was eaten as far back as the Bronze Age. It was one of the herbs identified as a food by archaeologists at the Sicilian settlement at Porth Killer.

The exceptional nutritional value of chickweed was mentioned in <u>The Useful Family Herbal</u> of 1788, which reports that it is good for the scurvy. Modern science has shown that chickweed is indeed very nourishing and would be useful for this very condition. We now know that this humble weed is high in vitamins and minerals and that its major plant constituents are Beta-carotene, Calcium, Magnesium, Niacin, Potassium, riboflavin, Rutin, Selenium, Vitamin C and Zinc. Chickweed is lovely to eat and can be either lightly steamed, where it can barely be distinguished from spring spinach, or raw mixed in with other salad leaves.

In his <u>Herbal</u> of 1597 John Gerard mentions chickweed as a medicinal herb he also goes to great pains to identify the different varieties of this plant. He says of chickweed (as a cure for suppurating wounds) - 'in a word,' (which, with Gerard always means a few words) 'it comforteth, digesteth, defendeth, and suppuateth very notably.' This is high praise indeed from this 'master of herbs'.

Chickweed water, which is lovely to drink and full of vitamins and minerals, is an old wives remedy for obesity. So absolutely… win win…

This herb of the moon is associated with the emotions and love and is worn (dried in a sachet of muslin) to improve a relationship.

Clover (Red): *Trifolium Pratense*

Hedgerow herb: common

Parts Used: Flower heads

Gathering: The flower heads are gathered between May and September

Actions:

Alterative

Anti-spasmodic

Depurative

Expectorant

Indications: Red clover will normalise the system it is therefore a very important addition to the holistic medicine chest. A spring tonic of clover is strongly recommended to restore vitality after the long winter months.

Red clover is a must for the treatment of skin conditions such as eczema and psoriasis.[4]

The expectorant action of this herb will help with any bronchial coughs including whooping cough.

Red clover is credited with the ability to restore fertility in women.

Clover is also useful as a relaxing tea to alleviate stress especially when mixed in equal parts with lime flowers and lemon balm.

Preparation and Dosage: Infusion: pour a cup of boiling water onto 1-3 tsp of the dried herb and infuse for 10-15 minutes this should be drunk three times a day.

Tincture: take 2-6mls three times a day.

Folklore, History and Kitchen Witch: Clover belongs to Venus, the goddess of love, so to attract new love or rekindle a love that already exists carry some clover flowers in your purse or pocket. To continue the link with Venus it is said that to dream of clover foretells a happy marriage.

Clover is a divinatory plant and many meanings have been given to the number of leaves found on a stem of clover, the most popular examples being, three leaves for the trinity; four for luck; five for fame; six for money and seven for prosperity.

---

[4] According to Hoffmann Red clover is particularly useful for the treatment of these conditions in children.

To dispel evil witchcraft or to discourage unwanted entities clover is tinctured in vinegar for three days and then sprinkled around the house. You can also carry clover on your person as a protection charm.

According to Lesley Gordon, Druids venerated Clover as a symbol of the earth, the sea and the heavens and Juliette De Baircli Levy remarks that herbalists often refer to it as a 'God given remedy'. Clover, it seems, is widely valued.

Phillips in his <u>Wild Food</u> says that, First Nation Americans eat clover in several ways; the Digger tribe cook moistened layers of it in a stone oven and the Apache boil it with dandelions, grass and pigweed. The Pomo tribe used to hold special clover feasts and dances in early spring to celebrate the appearance of this valuable source of food.

The leaves of clover can be cooked like spinach as a vegetable (however, this would mean a lot of work picking) also the leaves and flowers are a lovely addition to any salad.

Clover makes a soothing cream and an infusion of flowers can be used as a lightening hair rinse or as a mild bleach for freckles.

Dried clover flowers can be mixed with dried coltsfoot leaves and used as herbal tobacco.

Coltsfoot: *Tussilago Farfara*
Hedgerow herb: fairly common

Parts used: Dried flowers and leaves

Gathering: gather the flowers before they have fully opened during March and April. The leaves, which appear later than the flowers, are best collected for drying between May and June. Fresh leaves can be used throughout the summer and into the early autumn.

Actions:
Anti-catarrhal,
Anti-spasmodic
Anti-tussive
Demulcent
Diuretic
Expectorant

Indications: The anti-inflammatory effects of coltsfoot make it useful for all respiratory conditions. This plant can be used to ease the symptoms in cases of bronchitis (acute or chronic), whooping cough, asthma and irritating coughs of all kinds.

Coltsfoot is useful in the treatment of sinusitis because of its anti-catarrhal action. This herb is soothing when taken for throat conditions when it can be combined with red sage for increased potency.

The diuretic and demulcent effects of coltsfoot make it useful in cases of cystitis. Externally the leaves can be used as a compress to treat boils, ulcers or abscesses.

Preparation and dosage: Infusion: 1-2 teaspoons of the dried flowers or leaves to a cupful of boiling water infused for about 10 minutes, which should be drunk three times a day.

Tincture: take 2-4 ml of tincture three times a day.

Folklore, History and Kitchen Witch: Coltsfoot is a herb of Venus it is also sacred to the Irish goddess of fire and hearth Brighid, hence magically speaking, it is connected with love and passion, so if its love you wish to attract - you could do worse than carry a sachet of coltsfoot on your person. Before the introduction of matches the fluffy cottony down that is found under the leaves of coltsfoot was dipped in saltpetre and used as tinder, this practice seems to support the plants link to the fire goddess Brighid.

The high esteem with which this herb was held in the 19th century can be seen by the choice of Coltsfoot above all others to advertise the whereabouts of the local apothecary. The use of easy to recognise symbols was paramount in the days before widespread literacy and it was the leaves of coltsfoot that were painted on the doors of the local apothecary's shop and house. From this evidence it can be reasoned that Coltsfoot was universally accepted as an effective medicine in the 19th century.

The generic name *tussilago* comes from cough-wort the Latin *tussis* being a cough. This herb, once known as 'British tobacco', was recommended by some of the earliest known herbalists. Dioscorides, Galen and Pliny the Elder are amongst a great number of respected authorities both ancient and modern who have recommended the smoking of this herb as a cure for lung complaints. Modern science has borne out the reasons for the plants long-standing reputation and has, once more, proven what we already knew. We can now repeat with confidence and the backing of modern science that coltsfoot combines a soothing expectorant effect with an anti-spasmodic action and that this combination is enhanced by the plant's high levels of Zinc a mineral that has been shown to have anti-inflammatory effects.

Comfrey: *Symphytum Officinale*
Hedgerow herb: common

Parts used: Root and rhizome, leaf

Gathering: Dig the root in spring or autumn; the leaves can be collected all year round

Actions:
Astringent
Demulcent
Expectorant
Vulnerary

Indications: Comfrey is a powerful wound-healing herb effective both internally and externally.

Internally, Comfrey can be used to assist the healing of gastric and duodenal ulcers, hiatus hernia and ulcerative colitis. It is also a gentle and effectual remedy for diarrhoea and dysentery.

Where an irritable cough or bronchitis is present comfrey will be found to relieve the cough whilst helping expectoration.

A strong infusion of comfrey is useful as a mouthwash for bleeding gums or as a gargle for a sore throat.

Externally, comfrey is very effective when applied to bruising, sprains or strains. Superficial cuts and grazes can be treated very effectively with comfrey cream but care should be taken with deeper wounds as comfrey will seal the wound and any undetected deeper infection within the wound itself will fester and cause problems. It may be applied as a compress or poultice for any external ulcer, fracture or wound. It is very effective for the treatment of varicose ulcers.

Preparation and dosage: Infusion: a teaspoon of dried or a tablespoon of fresh herb to a cupful of water. Brew for 10-15 minutes drink a cupful three times a day.

Decoction: put 1-3 teaspoons of the dried root to each cup of water in a saucepan, bring to the boil and let it simmer for 10-15 minutes. This should be drunk three times a day.

Tincture: take 2-4 ml of the tincture three times a day.

Folklore, History and Kitchen Witch Comfrey is a herb of Saturn largely because both Saturn and comfrey are strongly associated with structure. The generic name *symphytum* is from the Greek *symphyo* 'to unite' and refers to the herbs long-standing reputation for healing broken bones and repairing internal injuries.

The Greek physician Dioscorides (40-90 AD), a well-known military physician of his day, documented the use of comfrey in his herbal and prescribed it for healing wounds, broken bones, respiratory and gastrointestinal problems. No doubt Dioscorides had plenty of opportunity to make use of comfrey during his career with the Roman army. Pliny the Elder, ever the scientist, reported that boiling Comfrey roots in water produced a sticky paste which glued pieces of meat together.

The 16th century the herbalist, Gerard, wondered at the virtues of comfrey in his Herbal.

In the 17th century comfrey's renowned medicinal qualities even found a place in theatre, Francis Baumont's comedy The Knight of the Burning Pestle (1607) mentions comfrey as a cure for broken bones, the script says: 'Go, get to your nightcap and the diet to cure your beaten bones, get thee some wholesome broth with sage and comfrey; a little oil of roses and a feather to 'noint thy back withall'.

In 1649 Culpepper reported in his Herbal that: 'this is a very common but a very neglected plant. It contains very great virtues'. He goes on to give an enormous list of conditions and symptoms that can be treated with comfrey.

Comfrey can also be used as a high nitrogen fertilizer for the garden. To make a simple but rather smelly feed take 2 lbs of comfrey leaves to 2 gallons of water and soak the leaves in the water for 4 to 6 weeks. Use neat or diluted with an equal volume of water.

For a almost smell free feed stack several lbs of comfrey leaves in a drum with a 1-2 inch hole drilled in the bottom, place a container underneath to catch the drips. Wait 10 -14 days a thick dark liquid can then be collected over several weeks. Top up with fresh leaves to continue the supply. Use diluted at about a 1 to 15-part ratio i.e. 1 pint to 2 gallons.

Dandelion: *Taraxacum Officinale*

Hedgerow herb: common

Parts used: Root or leaf

Gathering: Leaves can be collected anytime. Roots are best between June and August (they are bitterest then)

Actions:

Anti-rheumatic

Cholagogue

Diuretic

Laxative

Tonic

Indications: Dandelion is an excellent example of why herbal solutions to health problems are so in tune with the human body. Unlike most diuretics, which have the side effect of stripping the body of potassium dandelion is naturally rich in this mineral and therefore contains the antidote to its own side effect.[5] Clever old dandelion!

This herb can be safely used for any sort of oedema including bloating and water or fluid retention of any kind. Dandelion is especially effective when combined with yarrow and plantain for use in cases of oedema.

Dandelion also increases the flow of bile and may be used where inflammation or congestion of the liver or gall bladder is present; it is a specific in cases of congestive jaundice.

As a tonic, especially in the spring when the leaves can be picked fresh and added to salads, this herb will strengthen both the liver and kidneys after the long winter months.

Preparation and Dosage: Decoction: Place 1-2 teaspoons of root to each cup of water in a saucepan bring to the boil gently simmer for 10-15 minutes. Drink a cupful three times a day

Eat the leaves raw in salad, add a few leaves to your favourite green smoothie or juice them (best with other juices as some find dandelion slightly bitter)

Tincture: take 5-10 ml of the tincture three times a day.

Folklore, History and Kitchen Witch: Dandelion is under the dominion of Jupiter, the planet that rules the element of air. It therefore seems appropriate that the

---

[5] Lack of potassium aggravates any cardio-vascular problems that may be present and may cause muscular cramping.

seeds, with their little hairy parachutes, should be dispersed by the wind. Jupiter often rules plants that grow abundantly and dandelion is a particularly good example. Such is its power to multiply that a single root flowering in the spring is capable of propagating five new generations by the end of a good English summer. Which is excellent news for herbalists and not so good for gardeners!

This common weed has been used as a medicine and a food since the earliest times. It is mentioned in the first century by both Dioscorides, in his <u>Materia Medica</u> who referred to the roots as helpful for the liver, and Pliny, in his <u>Natural History</u>, who regarded the both the leaves and flowers as useful diuretics and digestive stimulants.

In the tenth century dandelion is mentioned in a manuscript written by the Arabian physician Avicenna(980-1037 A.D.) who used it to regulate menstruation and spoke of it as a sort of wild endive, under the name of Taraxacum.

The seventeenth century diarist John Evelyn recorded that dandelion was effective in the treatment of scurvy and says it was: 'thus excellent as an autumnal salad' he also reports that it was dandelion that 'the good wife Hecate' fed to Theseus.[6]

In 1649, Culpepper whose raison d'être was to widely disseminate the medicinal uses of native and locally available herbs, highly praises the dandelion and speaks of its popularity on the continent. This quote is also interesting because it highlights his cynicism of the English medical establishment at the time: 'You see here what virtues this common herb (dandelion) hath, and that is the reason the French and Dutch so often eat them in the Spring: and now if you look a little farther, you may see plainly, without a pair of spectacles, that foreign physicians are not so selfish as ours are, but more communicative of the virtues of plants to people'.

The name of the genus, Taraxacum, is derived from the Greek taraxos (disorder), and akos, (remedy) this certainly attests to the plant's ability to heal.

Its common name, dandelion, is from the French dent a lion (or translated tooth of the lion) due to either its resemblance to the sun (and by extension, Leo the lion, or its tiny little tooth like petals). The French also commonly and affectionately refer to the plant as pisenlit (i.e. wee the bed) presumably because of its powerful diuretic qualities.

According to Hopman, dandelion tea is said to increase psychic abilities because of the plant's ability to cleanse and rejuvenate.

---

[6] However this must have been a mistranslation on his part for Pliny the elder (23 AD – 79 AD) in his <u>Natural History Book 22 chapter44</u> tells us that it was sow thistle.

Echinacea: *Echinacea Angustifolia*
Garden herb

Parts used: Root and rhizomes

Gathering: The roots and rhizomes should be gathered in the autumn.

Actions:
Alterative
Anti-bacterial
Anti-fungal
Anti-inflammatory
Anti-microbial
Anti-viral

Indications: Echinacea boosts the immune system and is useful in cases of viral or microbial infection. According to James Wong it has been shown in many studies that if echinacea is taken as soon as the signs of colds or flu show themselves it will lessen the severity and duration of these conditions.

It is particularly useful for infections in the upper respiratory tract such as tonsillitis and laryngitis also for blocked sinuses.

Echinacea is indicated for putrid skin conditions such as boils and septicaemia where it can be taken internally and the tincture used as an external wash.

The tincture may be used as a mouthwash in the treatment of gingivitis or pyorrhoea.

Preparation and dosage: decoction: place 1-2 teaspoons of the root into a cup of water, bring to the boil and simmer 10-15 minutes. This should be drunk three times a day.

Tincture: take 1-4 ml of the tincture three times a day.

Folklore, History and Kitchen Witch: It seems that none of the early western herbalists knew this herb. Nevertheless, to omit it from this herbal on these grounds would seem remiss, as it is such an important component of any herbalist's medicine chest.

This was a herb of the Americas and the new world. The First Nation Americans were generous with their knowledge of medicine as was recorded by a the Spanish physician and botanist Nicolás Monardes (1493 –1588) who said: 'our Occidentall Indians doeth sende unto us many Trees, Plantes, Herbes, Rootes, Joices, Gummes, Fruites, Licours, Stones that are of greate medicinall vertues, in the whiche there bee founde, and hath been founde in them, verie greate effectes'

The earliest settlers in America found that the First Nation American Sioux and Comanche tribes were aware of echinacea's antiseptic properties and that they used the herb widely to treat snakebites, toothaches, sore throats and even smallpox. So important was this herb to the First Nation peoples that they even used it as an offering to the 'spirits'. The settlers, realizing the value of echinacea soon adopted the herb and brought it to Europe in the 1700's where it has been widely used as a herbal remedy ever since.

Elder: *Sambucus Nigra*

Hedgerow shrub: common

Parts used: bark, berries, flowers, and leaves

Gathering: The flowers are gathered in spring and early summer. The bark and berries in August and September.

Actions:

Bark-
Diuretic, Emetic, Purgative

Leaves-
Externally:
Emollient, Vulnerary
Purgative

Elderflowers
Anti-catarrhal, Diaphoretic

Elderberries-
Diaphoretic, Diuretic, Laxative

Indications: The leaves are used for wounds, bruising, sprains and chilblains.

The flowers are a specific remedy for the treatment of colds and influenza.

As an infusion used on sterile cotton wool or in an eye bath is extremely useful for cases of tired or inflamed eyes or where conjunctivitis or any other eye infection is present.

The flowers are especially valuable for the treatment of any catarrhal inflammation of the upper respiratory tract such as often exists in cases of sinusitis or hay fever. Catarrhal deafness also responds well to treatment with elderflowers.

Elderberries have similar properties to the flowers and can be used effectively for the same conditions. In addition the berries can be used for cases of rheumatism.

Preparation and dosage: Infusion: pour a cup of boiling water on to two teaspoons of the dried, or a tablespoon of the fresh, flowers. Drink a cupful three times daily.

Juice: boil fresh berries in a little water for 2 – 3 minutes then squeeze out the juice. To preserve the juice for a couple of weeks you should bring the juice to the boil and add 1 part honey to 10 parts juice. Take a shot glass full diluted with water three times a day.

Tincture: Take 2 – 4 ml of a tincture of the flowers or berries three times a day.

Ointment: To make a simple but effective ointment for the treatment of wounds, bruising sprains and chilblains: take 3 parts of fresh Elder leaves and heat them with 6 parts of melted Vaseline until the leaves are crisp. Strain out the plant material and store.

<u>Folklore, History and Kitchen Witch</u>: Elder belongs to Venus the goddess of beauty and love, it is not, therefore, surprising to find elderflowers are widely used in wish fulfilment spells and especially in love potions.

In 1644 the diarist John Evelyn said this of elder: 'If the medical properties of its leaves, bark and berries were fully known, I cannot tell what our countryman could ail for which he might not fetch a remedy from every hedge, either for sickness, or wounds.'

…. Or in the words of a suggestion passed on by Rafe Nauen: 'when in doubt, use elder'… a sentiment with which I wholeheartedly agree!

Elder is, without doubt, one of the most useful herbs in the medicine chest and there is evidence that it has been used as medicine since antiquity. Elder has been identified it as one of the herbs known to Hippocrates (460-370 BC). Although Hippocrates used this herb it is nowhere suggested that he introduced it to the Greek herbal canon, so it can be deduced that the use of elder goes back even further than his lifetime.

The Anglo-Saxon <u>Leech Book of Bald</u> mentions elder as one of the herbs to be administered to a patient suffering from 'in the water disease', whose symptoms included discoloured bluish nails and tearful eyes, the herbs were to be administered whist incantations were sung to 'quell the elf' and finally to bury it in the earth. The conjuration reads:

'I have wreathed round the wounds
The best of healing wreaths
That the baneful sores may
Neither burn nor burst,
Nor find their way further,
Nor turn foul and fallow.
Nor thump and throle on,
Nor be wicked wounds,
Nor dig deeply down;
But he himself may hold
In a way to health.
Let it ache thee no more
Than ear in Earth acheth.

"Sing also this many times,
'May earth bear on thee with all her might and main.'
—*Leech Book of Bald*

In former times in England a dryad, 'Elder Mother', Queen of all the elves, was said to live in the roots of the elder tree and it was customary to ask her permission before removing any part of her home.

The elder's connection with fairies and elves was widespread throughout Europe and there are many folk tales concerning the fair folk and elder. For example, it was rumoured that if a baby were put to sleep in a cradle of elder wood mischievous fairies would come and wake the infant by pinching it. Another tradition held that if one were to sleep under an elder tree on midsummer's eve, with any luck, they would see Queen Mab of the fairies and her entourage pass by. It was also understood that adding a few dried elderberries to an incense mix would attract fairies to any magical gathering … but be careful if you try this at home… fairies are full of mischief.

The tree is not only associated with fairies and elves but also with the hag or crone aspect of the triple goddess. This means, that in magical terms, the elder is connected with death and rebirth. This connection is reflected in its position in a 'tree calendar' that was constructed using evidence from various poetic sources by Robert Graves in the 1940's. In this thirteen month lunar calendar elder rules the very darkest part of the year between November 25th and December 21st. The last full moon in the year is widely known, in magical networks, as the elder moon and it is considered a very auspicious time for letting go of all regrets in time for the winter solstice when a new start can be made with the increase of the light. Witches were said to be able to turn themselves into elder trees when they wished to hide, possibly another reason to show this shrub a lot of respect!

This may be one reason why Traditional and New Age Travellers believe that it is extremely bad luck to burn elder because dreadful consequences will fall on those who do so, even by mistake!

A simple infusion of the leaves will act as an effective insecticide for the garden it may also be used to keep insects from the face and body.

Elderflowers and berries have been used for cosmetics since records began. The first century botanist, Pliny the Elder, recorded in his <u>Natural History</u> (book 24 chapter 25) that the berries were used to dye the hair in Roman times.

Today the flowers are used to make a fine lotion for the face and a soothing gel or wash for the eyes and when mixed with yoghurt they can be used as a facial mask to help to fade freckles and remove wrinkles.

For a really refreshing summer bath place a couple of heads of elderflowers in a muslin bag and hang it under the hot tap whist pouring the water. Mmmmm… gorgeous.

Elderflowers and berries find their way into many drinks, sweets and preserves and I have included a wealth of recipes for Elder in the recipe section.

Garlic: *Allium Sativum*
Garden plant: widely available

Parts used: Bulb
Gathering: Bulbs grown at home should be unearthed in September when the leaves start to die back. They should be stored in a cool dry place. Alternatively, garlic can be gathered all year round in any grocers or supermarket.
Actions:
Antiseptic
Anti-spasmodic
Anti-viral,
Cholagogue
Diaphoretic
Hypotensive.
Indications: Garlic is often seen only as a simple kitchen ingredient however it is also a most amazing medicine, which gives the body a great deal of support and protection against disease. It is almost without equal amongst plants as an anti-microbial agent, this means that it is effective against bacteria, alimentary parasites and viruses.

Garlic is particularly useful for lung problems and should always be considered when the respiratory system is under stress. Conditions such as bronchitis, respiratory catarrh, recurrent colds and influenza all benefit from treatment with garlic. It may also be useful in the treatment of whooping cough and as part of a regime for those with bronchitic asthma.

Garlic will act as a preventive for most infectious conditions both respiratory and digestive.

Taken over a long period of time garlic will reduce cholesterol levels and lower high blood pressure. It can also be used externally to treat ringworm.

Preparation and dosage: A clove should be eaten three times a day.

Folklore, History and Kitchen Witch: Garlic is under the dominion of Mars and it t is fitting that the god of war should rule a plant whose name, of Anglo-Saxon origin, is Gar (a spear) and Lac (a plant) or spear plant...

Garlic has been used as a medicine since time immemorial. According to Leslie Gordon garlic was known by the Chinese as early as 2000 BC and has been used medicinally by them ever since. Garlic is mentioned in a Sumerian clay tablet dating back more than 4,500 years. This may be the first written account of the herb and it names garlic in a list of dietary staples.

The first century Roman writer, Pliny the elder, claimed that the Egyptians honoured garlic as a deity at the taking of oaths and indeed garlic is mentioned in the Egyptian Ebers Papyrus (c.1550 B.C.) this is one of the world's oldest medical texts which lists literally hundreds of herbal remedies. Twenty-two of them include garlic as an ingredient. Pliny also attested garlic's continuing popularity as an effective cure all by ascribing sixty-one remedies to it in his <u>Natural History</u>.

In 1649 Culpepper included the wonders of garlic in his <u>Complete Herbal</u> where he claims that this ordinary kitchen item would: provoke the urine and women's courses, help the biting of mad dogs, and other venomous creatures; kill the worms in children, cut and void tough phlegm, purge the head, help the lethargy and be a good preservative against, and a remedy for, any plague, sore or foul ulcer'... this is indeed an altogether impressive list for this familiar vegetable.

It is common knowledge that garlic is proof against vampires and even, on occasion, the advances of unwanted lovers. Garlic's reputation as a herb of protection, which is also another nod to its planetary ruler Mars goes way back into antiquity. According to Theophrastus (371 -378 BC) garlic was left on piles of stones at crossroads as a supper for Hecate the 'changing woman' whose protection was eagerly sought by all. In his <u>Odyssey</u> Homer writes that the god Hermes gave garlic to Ulysses as an antidote to the evil magic of Circe, this highlights the use of garlic against dark magic. The use of garlic as a herb of protection has remained popular in neo-pagan circles largely because of this long held belief in its power against evil. Actually, should it be necessary to deter unwanted spirits of any kind you could do worse that hang Garlands of garlic around your doors and place bulbs or cloves of garlic on windowsills with a sprinkle of salt.

Garlic is a component of the very famous "Marseilles Vinegar" or "Four Thieves Vinegar". There are many variations on both the legend of the four thieves and the recipe for their vinegar, but briefly, and as it was told to me, the story surrounds four French men who plundered the homes of plague victims around Marseille in the 1600's and yet remained unaffected by the plague themselves. They were captured and, as the penalty for looting was death, they bargained for their lives by offering the magistrate the recipe for their vinegar. It is said that he happily accepted their offer and that they were spared. The recipe for this vinegar (or tincture) is included in the recipe section.

Herbalists now generally accept that garlic is an effective antiseptic. Louis Pasteur the French chemist began the first modern scientific research in 1858. Pasteur placed cloves of garlic in a Petri dish full of bacteria and observed that after a few days a bacteria-free area surrounded each clove. This research has been built upon and garlic has since been credited with killing 23 types of bacteria, including salmonella and staphylococcus. The bulb was in great demand for use as an antiseptic during both the First and Second World Wars. In 1916 the British government offered 1 shilling per pound (£2.64 at today's prices) for as much garlic as could be produced. During World War II, the Soviet army used garlic to prevent infections after they had run out of antibiotics, and garlic became known as 'Russian Penicillin'.

Ginger: *Zingiber Officinale*
Can be cultivated: widely available as a food item

Parts used: The rhizome
Gathering: Rhizomes may be harvested at any time, but it is best to gather ginger in the autumn when the leaves have died down. Ginger is usually sun-dried after harvesting to help preserve it, then stored in a well-ventilated, dry cupboard or in the fridge
Actions:
Carminative
Diaphoretic
Rubefacient
Stimulant.
Indications: This root's extremely valuable carminative effects make it an essential herb to have in both the kitchen and the medicine chest. Ginger is useful whenever there are nasty digestive problems such as colic, heartburn or flatulence.

Ginger root is effective in the treatment of both travel and morning sickness.

As a diaphoretic it can be taken when perspiration needs to be stimulated in feverish conditions.

Ginger is also an excellent stimulant for the peripheral circulation it can therefore be used effectively when there are any symptoms connected with poor circulation such as cramps and chilblains.

Ginger forms the base for many external rubs for muscle sprains and aching joints and you will find a recipe for a good home made massage oil in the recipe section.

Preparation and dosage: infusion: pour a cupful of water onto a teaspoonful of the chopped or bruised fresh root and let it steep for 5 minutes. Drink whenever needed.

Decoction: Use 1½ teaspoons of powdered or chopped dried root in a cup of water in a pan. Bring to the boil and simmer for 5-10 minutes. Drink as often as needed.

Folklore, History and Kitchen Witch: Ginger is a herb of Mars the god of war and therefore it is strongly connected with both protection and passion. A whole dried root will protect from evil spirits, bad dreams, and hag-riding if kept under the pillow.

Originating in India, ginger is mentioned in the earliest Sanskrit literature where it is known as Singabera. Ginger has been used as a medicine in India from Vedic period and is called maha-aushadhi, which means 'a great medicine'. The physicians of ayurveda considered ginger to be a wonderful carminative. The use of ginger as a digestive had reached China by 500 B.C. when Confucius, the Chinese philosopher, claimed he was never without ginger when he ate.

Ginger is also mentioned as an aphrodisiac in the most famous of Sanskrit texts, <u>Karma Sutra</u> so it is evident that, this Martian herb has a long-standing connection with passion. So if its passion you want… it is historically well established that a dash of ginger will heat up your love spells and you would be well advised to add dried ginger to love oils and powders to increase the heat. Grrrrrr…

Ginger was one of the first spices to find its way to the west along the spice route, where both the Greeks and Romans made extensive use of it. In the first century A.D. the Greek physician Dioscorides enjoyed pickled ginger imported from Eretria and he also recommended its use as a digestive stimulant in his <u>Materia Medica.</u>

The sixteenth century apothecary Nicholas Culpepper was also familiar with ginger reporting that: 'it helps digestion, warms the stomach, clears the sight, and is profitable for old men: heats the joints, and therefore is profitable against the gout, expels wind; it is hot and dry in the second degree'.

Hawthorn: *Crataegus Oxyacantha*
Hedgerow tree: common

Parts used: flowers and berries
Gathering: flowers should be gathered during May and the berries in September and October.
Actions:
Flowers:
Astringent
Nervine
Tonic.
Berries:
Astringent
Cardiac tonic
Diuretic,
Hypotensive.
Indications: Both the flowers and berries are astringent and may, therefore, be used in decoction for a sore throat. The flowers may be taken for palpitations, insomnia, anxiety and dizziness and are especially recommended when these symptoms are associated with the menopause.

The berries are one of the best tonic remedies known for the circulatory system and particularly for the heart. The berries have a normalising action, which balances the function of the heart. If the function of the heart is depressed hawthorn berries will act to energise it, if on the other hand the heart is too energetic the berries act to depress it. Hence, hawthorn berries will help to return the heart to its normal function in a gentle yet effective way. Hawthorn berries can be used for palpitations and can be safely administered long-term to strengthen the heart.

Preparation and dosage: Infusion: flowers: 1 tsp of the dried or 2 teaspoons of the fresh flowers to one cup of boiling water cover and brew for 10 minutes. Allow 2-3 cups a day. Berries: pour a cup of boiling water onto 2 tsp. of the berries and infuse for 20 minutes. This should be drunk three times a day over a long period. Tincture: take 2-4 ml of the tincture three times a day.

Folklore, History and Kitchen Witch: Hawthorn is a tree of Mars and again its name, from the Greek, seems very apt for a plant belonging to the god of war - *kratos*, meaning hardness, *oxus* (sharp), and *akantha* (a thorn) a hard sharp thorn... quite a weapon in the wrong hands.

The hawthorn has long been considered a tree of magical and religious importance and there are several long-standing limitations concerning human interaction with this tree. For example, it is considered extremely bad luck to bring hawthorn flowers in to the home and even though I think the flowers smell divine I dare not bring them in to this day because of the telling off I got from my grandmother for doing so when I was a little girl. It is also considered very bad luck to chop down or even damage an ancient hawthorn because in times gone by it was widely believed that fairy folk lived in and around them.

The most famous holy thorn is surely that of Glastonbury. According to tradition, Joseph of Arimathaea (possibly accompanied by the child Jesus) visited Glastonbury in the first century AD. Sometime later, after the crucifixion, Joseph returned to Glastonbury and made contact with the local druids hoping to spread the Christian faith. Whilst on this visit, it is said that Joseph thrust his staff (which had been gathered from the tree that had provided Christ's holy crown of thorns) into the ground at the bottom of Wearyall Hill where it promptly took root and burst into leaf. The locals believed that the holy thorn was the only one that bloomed twice a year once around Christmas time and once in springtime. And so the tree was clearly a miracle and sign of divinity to the people of Glastonbury who have ever since propagated successive generations of the 'Holy Thorn'.

Not all herbalists have given this story much credence Culpepper scoffed (as he is wont to do): 'As for the Hawthorn Tree at Glastonbury, which is said to flower yearly on Christmas-day, it rather shews the superstition of those that observe it for the time of its flowering, than any great wonder, since the like may be found in divers other places of this land; as in Whey-street in Romney March, and near unto Nantwich in Cheshire, by a place called White Green, where it flowers about Christmas and May.'

Culpepper may have been skeptical about the holy thorn but he was certainly not so dubious about the medicinal efficiency of hawthorn in general, which he recorded would treat a sizable list of ailments thus: The seeds in the berries beaten to powder being drank in wine, are held singularly good against the stone, and are good for the dropsy. The distilled water of the flowers stays the lask. The seed cleared from the down, bruised and boiled in wine, and drank, is good for inward tormenting pains.

In May time the hawthorn is part of the Beltaine rituals for love and fertility and is often linked to courtship and marriage. It is said that girls would attempt to secure a husband during the spring rites and would use love potions and charms to this ends. The hawthorn is connected with beauty as well as magic. A traditional rhyme reads:

> The fair maid who, on the first of May,
> Goes to the fields at the break of day,

And washes in dew from the hawthorn tree,
Shall ever after handsome be.

Lavender: *Lavendula Augustafolia(formerly Lavendula Officinalis)*
Garden herb: common

Parts used: the flowers

Gathering: the flowers should be collected just before they open between June and September.

Actions:
Anti-depressant
Anti-spasmodic
Carminative
Rubefacient.

Indications: A beautiful herb which has many uses in food, cosmetics and general well being. Lavender has been used since time out of mind for cases of nausea, indigestion and flatulence.

In cases of faintness lavender can be used instead of smelling salts.

This herb will help strengthen the nervous system it is therefore recommended for nervous exhaustion and debility and it is very effective for stress related headaches. Lavender should not be overlooked when treating the symptoms of low mood because it is a gentle tonic for the nerves.

A lavender bath at night followed by a cup of lavender tea works wonders in cases of insomnia especially when caused by stress. The essential oil has many external uses: mixed with honey it is an excellent treatment for burns after initial first aid with cold water and I have personally witnessed on several occasions a single drop of neat lavender oil in the ear cure a really nasty earache.

A drop of lavender oil neat on the skin is advised at the first sign of spots or pimples.

Lavender oil it is also useful as a component in a liniment for the treatment of rheumatic aches and pains the recipe for which is in the how to section. The essential oil is often added to disagreeable herbal ointments to improve their scent and also because of its long-standing reputation as an analgesic agent.

Preparation and dosage: infusion: add a cup of boiling water to a teaspoon of dried herb or two teaspoons of fresh herb and infuse for 10 minutes. Drink a cupful 3 times a day.

The oil can be rubbed on the skin, inhaled or used in baths. For perineal discomfort following childbirth 10 drops of lavender oil can be added to a sitz bath, which can be taken when necessary.

<u>Folklore, History and Kitchen Witch</u>: Lavender is under the dominion of the planet Mercury which presides over communication, the mind and the nervous system. Plants under the rule of mercury are often very ethereal with slender stems and feathery leaves and lavender is a good example of this. In 1647 W. Lilly in his <u>Christian Astrology</u>, reported that Mercurial herbs: 'have principle relation to the tongue or brain, lungs and memory; they dispel winde and comfort the animal spirits, and open obstructions.' All these qualities are in fact, present in lavender although the language used by Lilly seems rather archaic. Lavender has been in use since the earliest times and it is mentioned in the <u>regimen sanitatis Salernitanum</u> (c 12-13th C) a book of writings about the care of the body, which reports that: 'sage, castoreum, lavender, primrose, Nasturtium, and athanasia cure paralytic parts of the body'.[7]

During the twelfth century, washerwomen were ordinarily known in the north as Lavenderesses, from whence comes our name Laundress. It appears that the title was not gender specific as a 'Lavender man' is mentioned in the black book of Edward IV (1442 – 1483). This entry confirms lavender's enduring association with cleanliness as the lavender man in question was authorised to collect from the stores 'enough soap for the King's personal use'.

Lavender appears as a sign of homely hygiene in Izack Walton's <u>Compleat Angler</u> (1653) it says: 'I'll now lead you, to an honest ale-house, where we shall find a cleanly room, Lavender in the window, and twenty ballads stuck about the wall'.

Lavender is mixed with balm, violets, yarrow and rose petals in love potions and is one of the herbs that may be worn in an amulet to attract the love of a man.

Lavender is also one of the herbs connected to the goddess Hecate who is patroness to witches and sorcerers and also to her daughters Medea and Circe. It is said that an amulet of lavender will avert the evil eye.

In the 17th century lavender was included in nosegays to prevent the plague and to this end it was also included in the vinegar of the four thieves (see recipe section).

Mrs Grieve reports that during the Second World War the French Academy of Medicine used the oil for swabbing wounds and other antiseptic purposes. However, recent research has shown the antiseptic qualities of lavender to be rather low and variable from batch to batch. So if it's antiseptic you want you would be better off looking at cayenne, echinacea or garlic.

---

[7] The Salernitan regime of health... author unknown was written somewhere between the 12th and 13th centuries. The Scuola Medica Salernitana was the first medieval medical school in the cosmopolitan coastal south Italian city of Salerno it was the leading source of medical knowledge in Western Europe.

Marigold: *Calendula Officinalis*
Garden herb: easy to grow

Parts used: flower heads
Gathering: the heads are collected between June and September.
Actions:
Anti-fungal
Anti-inflammatory
Astringent
Cholagogue
Diaphoretic
Emmenagogue
Vulnerary

Indications: marigold is an extremely important herb for the treatment of skin problems. Its anti- inflammatory, anti-fungal and vulnerary actions mean that it should be considered whenever there is inflammation of the skin due either to infection or to physical damage.

Marigold is important in the nursery medicine chest as nappy rash often responds well to a cream of marigolds as does damage to the perineum torn in childbirth and sore nipples on nursing mothers.

It is very effective as a compress, poultice or ointment for external bleeding, bruising or strains. Consider marigold whenever a wound is slow to heal or skin ulcers are present.

A footbath of marigolds taken twice a day is a traditional remedy for athletes foot this is more effective when the footbath also contains 20 drops tea-tree oil.

Marigold is also very useful as an internal medicine it should be considered for gall-bladder problems and jaundice because of its cholagogue action. This property also makes the herb a simple remedy for indigestion. It is also useful where gastric inflammation is present, especially in the treatment of stomach or duodenal ulcers.

Marigolds have a time-honoured association with the uterus they act as a menstrual regulator and strengthen the whole reproductive system they should, therefore, be considered as a preliminary toner for the womb of women who wish to conceive.

The tonic effect of the flowers will help gently release delayed menstruation they will also ease menstrual pains in many cases.

<u>Preparation and dosage</u>: infusion: pour a cup of boiling water on to 1-2 tsp of the flowers. Infuse for 10-15 minutes. Take a cupful three times a day.

Tincture: take 2-4 ml of the tincture three times a day.

<u>Folklore, History and Kitchen Witch</u>: Marigold is a herb of the sun, which, according to Lilly the author of <u>Christian Astrology</u> (1647), means that: 'Their principal virtue is to strengthen the heart and comfort the vitals, to clear the eyesight, resist poison or to dissolve any witchery or malignant planetary influences'. Lilly mentioned marigold by name in his treatise and his contemporary, Culpepper, agreed with his astrological signature for this plant and added that it was under the sign of Leo.

Evidence shows that marigolds had been held in high esteem for centuries before Lilly and Culpepper's time and this is nowhere more obvious than in Macer's 10th century herbal. The earliest translation of this Latin herbal into English was by John Lelamoure, a schoolmaster from Hertford, in 1373. It is written in rhyme and says:

> "Golde [marigold] is bitter in savour
> Fayr and ʒelw [yellow] is his flowur
> Ye golde flour is good to sene
> It makyth ye syth [sight] bryth and clene
> Wyscely to lokyn on his flowris
> Drawyth owt of ye heed wikked hirores [humours].

I find it charming that the early herbalists such as Macer believed that not only did marigold flowers aid vision but also that the mere sight of them could cure a headache cause by the wicked humours.

The proper name of marigold (calendula) comes from the Latin Calends (new moon) some say that this is because it is said to bloom at the new moon, however, it is every bit as likely that the marigold's undisputed value in curing menstrual disorders led to this association with the moon's 28 day cycle.

The marigold has always been a popular herb in England where it has been grown from medieval times as much for a pot herb to be added to soups, stews, cakes and puddings as it was for medicine.

Culpepper draws attention to this facet of marigold saying: 'The flowers, either green or dried, are much used in possets, broths and drinks, being comfortable to the heart and spirits, and expelling any malignant or pestilential quality which might annoy them'. It seems we can deduce from this statement that Culpepper ascribed to the down to earth approach to healing of the great Hippocrates who said …'Let food be thy medicine, thy medicine shall be thy food'.

Bairacli Levy reports that the Arabs, whose thoroughbreds are admired the world over, like to feed marigolds to their swift horses because the flowers are esteemed for their benefit to the arteries and veins. This practice seems reasonable given marigold's astrological signature of the sun whose herbs strengthen the heart.

Further evidence of this Sun herbs ability to dissolve evil witchery is the practice of stinging garlands of marigolds outside the house to keep evil from entering the home.

Meadowsweet: *Spiraea Ulmaria*

Hedgerow herb (often found by water), common

Parts used: leaf and flower

Gathering: Between June and August when the flowers are fully open

Actions:
Anti-emetic
Antacid
Anti-inflammatory
Anti-rheumatic
Astringent
Stomachic

Indications: Meadowsweet is THE herb for the digestive tract, which it soothes and heals. It should, therefore, be considered for cases of excess acidity, nausea, heartburn, hyperacidity, gastritis or peptic ulceration.

It is a specific for diarrhoea especially in children because of its gentle astringent action.

Meadowsweet contains salicylic acid, which is a pain reliever related to aspirin, so this herb can be used to reduce fever and to relieve the pain of rheumatism in muscles and joints.

Preparation and dosage: infusion: use 1-2 teaspoons of the dried herb or 2-4 teaspoons of the fresh, to a cupful of boiling water and allow to steep for ten minutes. This can be drunk three times a day at least or when needed for digestive problems. Tincture: take 1-4 ml of the tincture three times a day

Folklore, History and Kitchen witch: Meadowsweet is under the dominion of Venus, which explains its association with weddings. It has been reported by various authors that in bygone days, on the wedding day itself, meadowsweet, which is also known by the country name of bridewort, was strung in garlands for the bride, strewn along both the bridal route and in the church itself and often woven into the bridesmaid's posies.

John Parkinson (1567-1600) mentioned meadowsweet as a strewing herb of royal favour claiming that: ' Queen Elizabeth of famous memory did more desire it than any other herbe to strew her chambers'. John Gerard in his herbal of 1597 also mentions meadowsweet in this context, saying: "The leaves and floures of meadowsweet farre excelle all other strowing herbs for to decke up houses, to strawe in chambers, halls and banqueting houses in the summertime, for the smell thereof makes the heart merrie and joyful and delighteth the senses."

Although the habit of strewing herbs has largely died out now I think there is much to be said for the practice if, for example, you are generally roughing it under canvas, where the sweet smell of the herbs is very welcome after a few days without a lot of water for washing. There is still evidence of herb strewing in Greece where church floors are strewn with bay leaves, which give off a sweet scent when they are walked on.

Gordon reports that the root of meadowsweet has been ground and used as a substitute for flour and that it was roasted as a vegetable and drunk as tea.

In the 14th century meadowsweet was called medwort or meadwort i.e. the mead or honey wine herb, the flowers being used to flavour not only mead but also many other wines and beers.

Mugwort: *Artemisia Vulgaris*
Hedgerow herb: very common

Parts used: leaves or root

Gathering: the leaves and flowering stalks should be gathered at flowering time, which is usually between July and September.

Actions:
Bitter tonic
Emmenagogue
Nervine tonic
Stimulant

Indications: Whenever a digestive stimulant is called for mugwort should be considered because it not only contains a bitter to stimulate the digestive juices but also carminative oil, which soothes the digestive process and relieves any bloating or trapped wind.

Kloss calls mugwort 'a safe and excellent medicine for female complaints'. Women of all ages may find mugwort a useful remedy in cases of suppressed menstruation because it can gently aid a return to the normal cycle. It is particularly useful when these symptoms are related to stress, as mugwort is also a mild nervine that is useful for easing tension and mild depression.

Preparation and dosage: Infusion: 1-2 teaspoons of the dried or 2-4 teaspoons of the fresh herb to each cup of boiling water. It is vey important to cover the pot as much of the plants active ingredients are in the steam which must not be allowed to escape the brew. Infuse for 10-15 minutes. A cupful should be drunk three times a day.

Tincture: take 1-4 ml of the tincture three times a day.

Folklore, History and Kitchen Witch: Mugwort is under the dominion of Venus and the strong association of this herb with the activity of the Womb bears this out.

In Anglo-Saxon times mugwort was used in the preparation of a herbal steam to cure those people and animals who had been shot by 'elf's arrows'. There are directions for the preparation of this steam, which is a time-honoured method of curing not only elf shot but also any other kind of demonic possession, in the Leech Book of Bald. This text, which is the oldest surviving leech book available, records that: the Anglo-Saxons took a huge quern stone, which had been in the fire on the hearth all day and placed on it the prepared herbs (in this case wallwort and mugwort) the herbs were scattered upon the stone, cold water was poured on to produce a steam and the patient was reeked with it. According to the manuscript the steam should be 'as hot as he can endure it'.

One cannot fail to see the connection between this burning of plant material, the burning of frankincense in Christian ceremonies, the burning of incenses in neo-pagan rites and the 'smudging' of participants and items with the smoke of white sage in First Nation American ceremonies.

Mugwort has also been identified as one of the herbs mentioned in the Anglo-Saxon *lay of the nine herbs*, which is a poem in praise of their most effective medicines. One surviving manuscript says of mugwort:

> "Eldest of worts
> Thou hast might for three
> And against thirty
> For venom availest
> For flying vile things,
> Mighty against loathed ones
> That through the land rove."

Harleian MS. 585.

The 1526 <u>Grete Herball</u> has an interesting use for mugwort in the nursery…it says: 'to make a child mery hange a bondell of mugwort or make smoke thereof under the chylde's bedde for it taketh away annoy for hem'.

Mugwort is one of the most popular herbs used in protection amulets. As early as the fifth century the <u>Herbarium of Apuleius</u> we read of mugwort: "and if a root of this wort be hung over the door of any house then may not any man damage the house." Pliny wrote of it as an amulet for travellers saying: 'the traveller or wayfaring man that hath mugwort tied about him feeleth no wearisomeness at all and he who hath it about him can be hurt by no poysonous medecines, nor by any wilde beaste, neither yet by the Sun itselfe'.

Mugwort has been used as an oracular herb John Chambers (1802-1871) reported in his <u>Book of Days</u> that on midsummer's eve: 'Young women sought for what they called pieces of coal, but which in reality were certain hard, black, dead roots, often found under the living mugwort, designing to place these under their pillows, that they might dream of their lovers'.

Mugwort is also used by some neo pagans to cleanse and refresh all magical or healing items by either by smudging or by washing the item in a strong infusion. This is especially important to maintain the clarity of items used for scrying such as crystal balls or tarot cards.

Nettle: *Urtica Dioica*
Hedgerow herb: very common

Parts used: Ariel parts
Gathering: collect when the flowers are in bloom
Actions:
Astringent
Diuretic
Tonic
Indications: Full of iron and Vitamin C nettles are simply a must have for human and animal health. This herb when taken regularly will strengthen and support the whole body. They are a superb tonic for the spring months.

Nettles are indicated for the treatment of anaemia because of their high iron content.

Nettles are a specific in cases of childhood eczema and should be used for all manifestations of this condition. They may be employed wherever there is haemorrhage in the body because of their astringency. Nettles are soothing to the urinary tract in cases of cystitis.

Preparation and dosage: Infusion: use 1-3 teaspoons of dried or 2-6 teaspoons of the fresh herb to each cup of boiling water. Brew for 5-10 minutes and take a cupful 3 times a day.

Tincture: take 1-4 ml of the tincture 3 times a day.

Folklore, History and Kitchen Witch: Nettles are under the rule of Mars the planet of passion and war and rather appropriately the proper name of nettle, urtica, is from the latin uro which means to burn or hurt.

It is common understanding that it was the Romans who introduced at least one variety of nettles to the British Isles. Tradition runs that certain Roman soldiers, upon hearing that the cold in England was unbearable, brought nettle seeds with them to ensure that they would have a ready supply of nettles with which to make rubbing oils to keep themselves warm. As evidence of this practice we have a prescription, that may date as far back as the Roman occupation of Britain (43 AD-410 AD), which runs: "Take nettles, and seethe them in oil, smear and rub all thy body therewith; the cold will depart away."

As testament to its enduring popularity as a healing plant the nettle is another of the herbs mentioned in the Ley of the Nine Herbs where it is called "wergulu".

In a Christian context, it is said that Saint Patrick himself blessed the nettle because it was useful for man and beast.

The Scottish poet Thomas Campbell (1777 – 1844) wrote of the many uses of nettles in one of his letters from Algeria, which were published in the New Monthly Magazine as 'letters from the south'. He says: 'In Scotland I have eaten nettles, I have slept in nettle sheets, and I have dined off a nettle tablecloth. The young and tender nettle is an excellent potherb, and the stalks of the old nettle are as good as flax for making cloth. I have heard my mother say that she thought nettle-cloth more durable than any other species of linen'.

Nettles were not only used for cloth making but also for the production of paper and Mrs Grieve tells us that the French have collected considerable quantities of nettles for this purpose although she does comment that more research is needed to perfect the process.

Nettles are a fantastic resource for the forager they can be used for food, drinks and cosmetics having a reputation for strengthening and conditioning the hair. All in all nettles have simply amazing heath benefits as one traditional rhyme relates:

> 'If they should eat nettles in March
> And drink mugwort in May
> So many fine maidens
> Would not go to the clay'.

So it is the wisdom of our forbears that urges us to eat our greens and drink the bitter herbs for our own self-preservation. We could do worse than heed their advice.

Peppermint: *Mentha Piperita*
Garden herb

Parts used: Arial parts
Gathering: The plant is collected just before it flowers
Actions:
Analgesic
Anti-emetic
Anti-spasmodic
Antiseptic
Aromatic
Carminative
Diaphoretic
Nervine

Indications: The carminative effect of peppermint is well known and for good reason as it is a safe and effective remedy for all digestive problems. Peppermint has a relaxing effect on the visceral muscles in the gut it has anti-flatulent properties and stimulates the secretion of both bile and digestive juices. These actions make peppermint a must for colic, indigestion, trapped wind and associated conditions. It can also be given for migraine headaches that are associated with the digestive tract.

Peppermint is useful for the treatment of morning sickness in pregnancy, travel sickness and any other kind of nausea. The symptoms of Crohn's disease and ulcerative colitis can also be effectively relieved by the use of peppermint.

Peppermint is customarily administered when fever is present especially for colds and flu. It is a component of the very effective traditional triad of herbs that is used to relieve the symptoms of flu, peppermint being mixed with elderflower and yarrow in equal parts.

As an inhalant it can give temporary relief from nasal catarrh.

Its tonic effect on the nervous system is widely praised as it greatly eases any kind of anxiety, tension or hysteria.

It is a must for women whose periods are painful and distressing as it gently relieves the symptoms and relaxes the associated tension.

Preparation and dosage: Infusion: use 2 teaspoons of dried or 4 teaspoons of fresh herb to each cup of boiling water. Infuse for 10 minutes. This can be drunk as often as desired.

Tincture: take 1-2 ml of the tincture three times a day

Folklore, History and Kitchen Witch: All the mints are under the dominion of Venus.

Gerard's much enamoured with mint in general saying that it is 'marvellous wholesome for the stomacke' which is no word of a lie. He also informs us that it stoppeth the cofing up of blood, being given with water and vinegar as Galen teacheth'. Clearly then, Gerard had a copy of Galen's herbal which he used for reference. Culpepper is no less enthusiastic about mint and he also refers to an earlier authority: 'Dioscorides, he says, 'saith it hath a healing binding and drying quality and therefore that the juice taken in vinegar stays bleeding. As can be seen although both men refer to different teachers their conclusions are the almost the same. References to the works of the great founders of medicine is a common theme in old herbals showing how these men repeatedly based their knowledge of herbal medicine on the experience of their ancestors.

Mint is one of the herbs whose name has distinct mythological roots. The legend begins around the river Cocytus, which is one of the five rivers that surround the underworld. It was here that the naiad, Minthe dwelt. The story runs thus: When Persephone discovered that her husband, Hades, had dazzled Minthe, with his golden chariot pulled by four black horses and that the naiad was about to succumb to his amorous advances, she metamorphosed poor Minthe into the herb that has borne her name ever since.

The association of mint with the underworld explains why, in ancient Greece, Mint was use in funerary rites.

Plantain: *Plantago Major*

Hedgerow herb: very common

Parts used: Arial parts

Gathering: collect during flowering during the summer months.

Actions:
Astringent
Demulcent,
Diuretic
Expectorant

Indications: This herb contains vitamins C and K and the minerals zinc and silica.

It is very effective in the treatment of all catarrhal conditions but especially those of the lungs and gut. Plantain is a specific for the treatment of infection of the middle ear or glue ear.

Plantain is very useful as an expectorant in troublesome coughs. It is taken internally for asthma and bronchitis.

It's astringency helps with cases of diarrhoea or haemorrhoids.

Its diuretic properties along with its astringency helps cases of cystitis where there is bleeding.

Preparation and dosage: Infusion: Take 2 teaspoons of dried or 4 teaspoons of fresh herb to each cup of boiling water. Infuse for 10 minutes. Take a cupful 3 times a day.

Tincture: take 2-3 ml of the tincture 3 times a day.

Ointment: an ointment is useful for the treatment of haemorrhoids and cuts.

Folklore, History and Kitchen Witch: Plantain is under the dominion of Venus. Plantain is yet another of our herbs mentioned in the Anglo-Saxon Lay of the Nine Herbs where it appears as waybroad. It is a component of the salve for flying venom, which appears in the *lacnunga* (the earliest surviving source of Anglo-Saxon medicine). The recipe reads: "A salve for flying venom. Take a handful of hammer wort (pellitory of the wall) and a handful of maythe (camomile) and a handful of waybroad (plantain) and roots of water dock, seek those which will float, and one eggshell full of clean honey, then take clean butter, let him who will help to work up the salve melt it thrice: let one sing a mass over the worts, before they are put together and the salve is wrought up."

As you can see this recipe or at least some of its additions relating to the mass date it to post 579 when the first Roman Christians arrived in Kent. The person who recorded this was probably a Christian cleric, no doubt, acting upon the belief that the Christian incantations would strengthen the medicine. This prescription was either transcribed from earlier writings that have been lost or may have based on oral traditions.

Plantain was a herb much used in the making of amulets, especially those for the safety of the journeyman, whom it is said, it protects against the hidden dangers of travel - such as snake bites and insect stings. In Ireland it is associated with the patron Saint St. Patrick, - interestingly, Saint Patrick is also associated with averting snakes.

Later the Pilgrim Fathers introduced plantain to the New World Jocelyn reports that: 'the Indians called this familiar weed "Englishman's Foot" as though it were produced by their treading'. Evidently those First Nation Americans soon saw the worth of the downtrodden plantain for in the 1930's Kloss called plantain an old-fashioned herb' and reported that 'the Indians used it to a great advantage.'

Raspberry: *Rubus Idaeus*

Hedgerow herb (often found in gardens)

Parts used: leaves and fruits

Gathering: the leaves can be gathered all thorough the growing season.

Actions:
Astringent
Parturient
Refrigerant
Tonic

Indications: This beautiful herb has a long-standing relationship with the womb and especially with the wombs of pregnant women. The leaves strengthen and tone the tissues of the womb thereby assisting contractions and checking any uterine bleeding during labour. The herb should be taken throughout pregnancy, during labour and for two or three weeks after the birth to help contract the uterine muscles so they can regain their former shape.

Its astringency makes this herb useful in loose conditions such as diarrhoea and leucorrhoea. Mouth ulcers, bleeding gums and inflammation of the mouth can all be successfully treated with raspberry leaves. This herb will help soothe sore throats as a gargle.

Preparation and dosage: infusion: 1-2 teaspoons of the dried or 2-6 teaspoons of the fresh herb to each cup of boiling water. Infused for 10-15 minutes. This brew may be drunk freely

Tincture: Take 2-4 ml of the tincture 3 times a day.

Folklore, History and Kitchen Witch: Raspberry is a herb of Venus and indeed without it many a woman would have suffered a great deal more in childbirth. In Hellenistic Troy raspberry was linked to both fertility and young children in the story of Ida, the nymph who was nursemaid to baby Zeus. Legend has it that Ida, whilst picking the snow-white berries of the raspberry bush for her charge, pricked her finger. Naturally this led to the berries being stained red for all eternity. It follows logically then that the Latin name for raspberry, *rubus idaeus*, means "bramble bush of Ida."

Raspberries are both delicious and nutritious one cup of raspberries contains about 40% of your daily needs for vitamin C, 10% of your daily needs of iron as well as numerous other vitamins an minerals which explains why this fruit is so popular in the kitchen where it is a favourite candidate for winter preserves.

Rose Hips: *Rosa Canina*

Hedgerow herb: Very common

Parts used: the fruit (hips) of the wild rose.

Gathering: The hips are collected in the autumn

Actions:

Astringent

Diuretic

Laxative

Nutrient.

Indications: The hips of the common dog rose contain one of the most generous amounts of vitamin C in the entire British flora. They should be used whenever this vitamin is called for.

This fruit will strengthen the body's defences against infections especially against colds. They are also appropriate for the treatment of general debility and exhaustion. Rose hips are a wonderful spring tonic. They are also useful for cases of constipation and gall bladder problems.

Preparation and dosage: Decoction: Place 2½ teaspoons of the cut hips in a saucepan with a cup of water. Cover the pan, bring to the boil and simmer for 10 minutes. This decoction can be taken freely.

Tincture: Take 2-4 ml of the tincture 3 times a day.

Syrup: you will find a recipe for rose hip syrup in the recipe section. This can be taken quite freely.

Folklore, History and Kitchen Witch: Roses are under the dominion of the moon and they have been with the human race since the very earliest times. We know this because an archaeological dig run by Sir Leonard Wooley recorded that 5,000 years ago the Sumerian King Sargon returned to his country with vines, figs and roses following a successful campaign. The very act of returning from a foreign war with these plants shows that King Sargon valued roses enough to consider them a symbol of his victory.

The rose was still in popular use in roman times and Pliny lists 32 medicines that can be prepared from roses in his Natural History.

Gerard attests to the high esteem that rose hips had in 16th century culinary circles, he says: 'the fruit when it is ripe maketh the most pleasant meats and banketting dishes as tartes and such like' the making of which he hands over to 'the cunning cooke and teethe to eate them in the riche man's mouth'.

In England, the humble rose hip really came into its own during the Second Wold War when rose hips for homemade syrups were collected by school children organised by the local Women's Institutes. So popular was this syrup that it was sold commercially in the UK after the war by a company called Delrosa. English children were paid 3d per lb for rosehips harvested in the autumn to be made into rosehip syrup by the company that was based in Wallsend (near Newcastle). For many years after the war, Delrosa Rose Hip Syrup was supplied for babies at National Health baby clinics throughout the UK. Indeed, I remember it well and can report that it was truly delicious!

Wartime children collecting rosehips

Sage: *Salvia Officinallis*
Garden herb: common

Parts used: leaves
Gathering: gather leaves in May or June shortly before flowering
Actions:
Antiseptic
Astringent
Carminative,
Emmenagogue
Perspiration inhibitor
Indications: Sage, (red sage if you can get it is the best for medicinal use) is considered to be a specific for the treatment of inflammations of the mouth, throat and tonsils especially when infection is present. It can be used internally and as a mouthwash for conditions such as inflamed and bleeding gums (gingivitis) or any inflammation in the mouth. It is also an excellent treatment for mouth ulcers.

An infusion of sage is a must for any kind of sore throat and this treatment benefits from the addition of a sage gargle to relieve the pain.

For cases of indigestion, especially after eating rich foods, it is recommended that sage tea is taken for its carminative effects. Sage is very good for the whole digestive tract and will stimulate the flow of bile and the functioning of the pancreas and liver.

If, following the birth of a child, overproduction of breast milk is a problem sage is recommended to reduce the flow and ease the pain of breast engorgement.

Sage's action as a perspiration inhibitor may give it some use to stop the hot flushes that accompany the menopause, however, it needs to be combined with other herbs so that the hormone balance can be addressed. It is, after all, no use just taking care of the symptoms whilst leaving the cause untreated.

Preparation and dosage: Caution! This herb is a very powerful emmenagogue and so medicinal use should be avoided during pregnancy.

Infusion: 1-2 teaspoons of the dried or 2-4 teaspoons of the fresh herbs to each cup of boiling water. Infuse for 10 minutes and drink three times a day.

Tincture: take 2-4 ml of the tincture three times a day

Mouthwash: place ½ litre (1 pt.) of water in a pan and add to it 2 teaspoonfuls of dried or 4 teaspoons of fresh herb. Cover, bring to the boil then let it stand for 15 minutes. Gargle several times a day for 5 -10 minutes. Folklore, History and Kitchen Witch: According to Culpepper sage is under the dominion of Jupiter, which is the planet that is considered to be the healer and ruler of the higher mind. Strangely enough, the relationship between Sage, the head in general and the memory in particular is often recorded in early herbals. In his <u>Theatrum Botanicum</u> (1640) Parkinson says that: 'sage is of excellent good use to helpe the memory by warming and quickening the senses'.

Gerard wrote of it, "Sage is singularly good for the head and brain, it quickeneth the senses and memory, strengtheneth the sinews, restoreth health to those that have the palsy, and taketh away shakey trembling of the members."

The name of the genus *salvia* is derived from the Latin *salvere*, to be saved, in reference, I think, to the high status of this plant as a healer. Indeed, this plant has been highly regarded as a medicine since the earliest times. It is mentioned in many of the existing translations from the Anglo-Norman era of Macer's herbal, including the earliest extant English translation of 1373, which says of sage:

> 'Why of seknesse deyeth man,
> Whill sawge [sage] in gardeyn he may han'.

The idea of sage bestowing immortality was clearly commonplace around that time for in the <u>regimen sanitatis Salernitanum</u> we find this verse, which is clearly attempting to be more realistic about the herb's medicinal powers:

> Why should a man die in whose garden grows sage?
> Against the power of death there is not medicine in our gardens
> But Sage calms the nerves, takes away hand
> Tremors, and helps cure fever.
> Sage, castoreum, lavender, primrose,
> Nasturtium, and athanasia[8] cure paralytic parts of the body.
> O sage the savior, of nature the conciliator!

In a Christian context, as we have seen with nettles and hawthorn and as we will see with St John's wort, early Christians saw the advantage of associating herbs with their saints and sage is no exception. The herb became enshrined in Christian legend: it is said that the Virgin Mary herself blessed the plant when it provided a safe haven for her as she escaped from the soldiers of Herod with the baby Jesus. She bestowed her blessing saying: 'from now to eternity you will be the favorite flower of mankind. I give you the power to heal man of all illness and save him from death as you have done for me.'

Presumably, up until the birth of Christ, the plant had managed quite well without the Virgin's blessing. Indeed, Hippocrates (460 -370 BC) knew its worth as he prescribed sage as a remedy for lung diseases and gynaecological disorders.

---

[8] Tansy

More recently my grandmother somehow knew and often repeated the old adage that the wife ruled the house when sage flourished in the garden.

St John's Wort: *Hypericum Perforatum*
Wild herb: reasonably common

Parts used: Parts above the ground
Gathering: The plant should be collected when in flower.
Actions:
Anti-inflammatory,
Astringent
Sedative
Vulnerary
Indications: St John's wort works as an effective sedative and pain reducer when taken internally. It therefore has a place in the treatment of anxiety, low mood, Neuralgia and similar complaints. This herb should always be considered for cases of fibromyalgia, sciatica and rheumatic pain.
The tetchiness and fretfulness caused by menopausal problems can be eased with this wonderfully calming herb. Externally the oil or lotion is a beneficial anti-inflammatory and healing remedy, which can be used on bruises, mild burns and varicose veins. Furthermore, and without hyperbole it can be stated that Saint John's wort oil is nature's perfect answer to sunburnt skin.

Preparation and dosage: Infusion: Take 1-2 teaspoons of dried or 2-4 teaspoons of fresh herb to one cup of boiling water. Infuse for 10-15 minutes. Drink a cupful three times a day.

Tincture: take 1-4 ml of the tincture three times a day.

Folklore and Kitchen witch: St. John's wort is a herb of the Sun and it is said to be at the zenith of its power on 24th of June, which is both the feast of St John and midsummer's day. This date is, of course, also very close to the summer solstice, which explains both its appropriation by the Christian saint and the relationship between St. John's wort and midsummer in neo-pagan circles.

Robert Chambers (1802-1871) recorded in his Book of Days that: 'The people also gathered on this night (midsummer's eve) the rose, St. John's wort, vervain, trefoil, and rue, all of which were thought to have magical properties. By tradition it was on the day of the 'feast of Saint John' that garlands of St John's wort and other flowers were hung at doors and windows to ensure protection for the occupants. So great was the protection of this wort that a house that had it hung above the door was considered to be safe from thunder, lightening and fire; and neither evil witches or the devil could cross the threshold.

St John's wort's remarkable protection abilities are recognised in this traditional rhyme:

> St John's wort doth charm all the witches away
> If gathered at midnight on the Saint's holy day
> Nor devils nor witches have then power to harm
> The man that doth gather this plant for a charm
> Rub lintels and posts with this red juicy flower
> No tempest nor thunder shall then enter your door.
>
> (Author unknown)

Gerard called the oil 'a most pretious remedie for deep wounds and those that are thorow the body, for the sinues that are prickt, or any wound made with a venomed weapon' ... he was obviously impressed. As was Culpepper who recorded that St John's wort was 'by no means least valuable for its efficacy in the cure of wounds, hurts, or bruises, by being boiled in wine and drunk'.

Wormwood: *Artemisia Absinthum*
Hedgerow herb: very common

Parts used: leaves or flowering tops

Gathering: May to September preferably when flowering is almost done

Actions:
Bitter tonic
Anthelmintic
Anti- inflammatory
Carminative

Indications: This common wayside herb stimulates and strengthens the whole digestive process. It is very effective in the treatment of heartburn or other manifestations of indigestion.

As its common name suggests this herb is effective in the treatment of worms particularly thread and roundworms.

Wormwood is a good general tonic and is useful for many diverse maladies. It will help the body deal with fever and infections.

Preparation and dosage: Warning - this brew is bitter!

Infusion: 1-2 teaspoons of the dried or 2-4 teaspoons of the fresh herb to each cup of boiling water. Infuse for 10-15 minutes. Take a cupful 3 times a day.

Tincture: Take 1-4 ml of the tincture 3 times a day.

Folklore, History and Kitchen Witch: Wormwood is governed by Mars. Its generic name is derived from the Greek goddess Artemis. As testament to the value given by classical herbalists to of this group of herbs an early translation of the Herbarium of Apuleius (Circa 550 – 625) states that: 'Of these worts that we name Artemisia, it is said that Diana did find them and delivered their powers and leechdom to Chiron the Centaur, who first from these Worts set forth a leechdom, and he named these worts from the name of Diana, Artemis, that is Artemisias.'

Presumably, Artemis gave Chiron the herbs dedicated to her so he could try them on himself...Chiron the centaur was a Greek God renowned for his healing skills and art as a physician. Nevertheless, when poor Chiron was accidentally shot in the knee by his friend Hercules with an arrow poisoned with the venom of the hydra he was unable to successfully treat the wound. After this incident Chiron became known as the 'wounded healer'.

The Bible often references wormwood usually in relation to its intense bitterness. In Proverbs V King Solomon says: Mind not the deceit of a woman. For the lips of a harlot are like a honeycomb dropping, and her throat is smoother than oil. But her end is bitter as wormwood, and sharp as a two-edged sword...What an old cynic... maybe he was just unlucky in love?

And whilst of the subject of the relationship between love and wormwood, Mrs Grieve sourced a lovely old love charm in her <u>Modern Herbal</u> it runs thus: 'On St. Luke's Day, take marigold flowers, a sprig of marjoram, thyme, and a little *Wormwood*; dry them before a fire, rub them to powder; then sift it through a fine piece of lawn, and simmer it over a slow fire, adding a small quantity of virgin honey, and vinegar. Anoint yourself with this when you go to bed, saying the following lines three times, and you will dream of your partner "that is to be":

'St. Luke, St. Luke, be kind to me,
In dreams let me my true-love see'.

Wormwood has always been associated with visions in one-way or another and Wormwood and debilitating alcoholic beverages seem to go hand in hand. Jeremiah in his lamentations complains: 'He hath filled me with bitterness: he hath inebriated me with wormwood'. Of course, this may not mean that he had actually drunk any thing with wormwood in it but rather that it just that it felt like he had. Pliny the elder makes numerous references to wormwood as flavouring for alcoholic beverages and it is well known that it was once used to flavour beer in the absence of hops. Wormwood is also an ingredient in Pernod and Vermouth but it is as a vital component of the, very naughty, absinthe that wormwood is best known.

Yarrow: *Achillea Millefolium*
Hedgerow herb: very common

Parts used: leaves, flowers and stalks

Gathering: the plant is at its zenith between June and September

Actions:
Antiseptic
Astringent
Diaphoretic
Diuretic
Hypotensive
Styptic

Indications: Yarrow is yet another humble plant with huge healing powers. As a diuretic and antiseptic it is useful for the treatment of urinary infections such as cystitis.

As a diaphoretic is knows no equal in reducing fevers especially those associated with colds and flu.

Yarrow can help lower high blood pressure and is a specific for the treatment of thrombotic conditions associated with high blood pressure.

Used externally yarrow is a fine treatment for wounds and its astringency helps staunch bleeding.

Preparation and dosage: Infusion: 1-2 teaspoons of the dried or 2-4 teaspoons of the fresh herb to a cup of boiling water. Steep for 10-15 minutes. Take a cupful three times a day. If fever is present drink a cupful every hour.

Tincture: Take 2-4ml of the tincture three times a day.

Folklore, History and Kitchen Witch: Yarrow belongs to Venus and has strong associations with love spells. One such spell appears in Mrs Grieve's Modern Herbal: To dream of your future spouse, sew an ounce of Yarrow up in flannel bag and place it under the pillow before going to bed. Then repeat the following words:

'plant recognition: medicinal uses: history/folklore: Thou pretty herb of Venus' tree; thy true name it is Yarrow;

Now who my bosom friend must be, pray tell thou me to-morrow.'

Yarrow's use as a divinatory herb was recognised in ancient China where the 3,000 year old I-Ching oracle used 50 yarrow stalks to determine the hexagram that foretold whether the omens were auspicious or not.

As can be seen, Yarrow has been known since oldest times, and the archaeological record bears this out for yarrow was one of the ten herbs whose pollen was identified at Shanidar IV, a Neanderthal flower burial of northern Iraq, dated 60,000 BC. Although we can only guess why those specific flowers were there, it is nevertheless fair to say that it was no accident and that, therefore, yarrow must have had some significant meaning for the occupant of that particular grave.

The generic name for Yarrow *achillea* is a reference to this herb's mythological associations with Achilles. Pliny the elder recounts that: 'Achilles too, the pupil of Chiron, discovered a plant, which heals wounds, and which, as being his discovery, is known as the "achilleos'. Others say that it was Chiron who taught Achilles to use yarrow to treat wounds caused by iron.

Either way as late as the 1930's Mrs Grieve reported that: 'Yarrow was formerly much esteemed as a vulnerary, and its old names of Soldier's Wound Wort and Knight's Milfoil testify to this. The Highlanders' she says 'still make an ointment from it, which they apply to wounds.'

The How To Section

In this section you will learn how to: Gather and dry various plant materials, make herbal teas and decoctions, tinctures, compresses, poultices, infused oils, simple creams and lotions.

Section one: Gathering and drying plant materials

Gathering herbs

The practice of gathering your herbal simples is, believe it or not, part of the healing process itself. Whilst collecting herbs flowers and fruits from any countryside hedgerow one cannot fail to feel more intimately connected to Mother Earth. One becomes more aware of the abundance of nature and our dependence on her bounty in ways that simply popping to the shop will never satisfy. Collecting and preserving food and medicine whilst there is a glut can be a meditation, an acknowledgement that nature has a pattern, a cycle and a rhythm of which we are all a part. Preparing for times of need is indeed an ancient ritual that gives each of us a warm glow of satisfaction because we know in the depths of our being that we are learning some of the earliest wisdom relating to our symbiotic relationship with nature

Gathering plants and roots the process overseen by a sage
(*Apuleius Platonicus* herbal ca. 1200)

Where to collect

Although many herbs grow in abundance on roadsides or urban waste lands it is sensible to try and avoid picking them in very polluted environments. It is also good to be aware that many famers spray their crops with the most disgusting pesticides and other chemicals and that these will end up in your herbal preparations if you pick herbs or fruits from places where these chemicals have been used. Just use your common sense and intuition to feel if the herb you see is growing in a good place. With some practice you can feel the vibration of the plant by using your hands to sense its energy field (this is about six inches to a foot away from the plant)… they really can talk to you!

When to collect

Science has now confirmed what herbalists have always known i.e. that the active properties of plant materials are highest just after the period of most vigorous growth. Bearing this in mind it is a good rule of thumb to say that:

- The barks of trees should be collected as the sap rises in the spring
- The leaves should be gathered just before the plant bursts into flower
- The flowers should be gathered the day after they flower if possible, but do make sure you get to them before they go over
- The roots should preferably be dug in the autumn or in an emergency in the spring before the aerial growth of the plant has really got going.

As a caveat to the above advice, I would like to add that I have on many occasions collected herbs when I have needed them, well out of the range of the above suggestions and have found the herbs to work perfectly well. I can't help but feel that we should not be too constricted by what is scientifically right but rather work with what we have. So if you see yarrow nestled in the lawn in winter and you need a flu remedy go ahead and pick it … that's what it's there for!

It is important to gather leaves and flowers that you intend to dry when their has been no rain for a couple of days and when the sun has been shining since daybreak. Wait until the dew has dried so that there is no moisture on the leaves as this is often the cause of mildew on your herbs but don't wait too long or the sun will dry the oils in the leaves.

Take the best leaves, flower or roots you can find and always thank the plant for its gift to you. Use secateurs or sharp scissors when cutting leaves and be sure not to damage the mother plant.

Drying plant materials

Dry Herbs leaves, stems and flowers either by spreading them in loose single layers on a flat surface away from too much dust (Wire cooling racks are useful for this process because they allow the air to circulate freely) or by hanging in loose bunches on an overhead line. If you have loose leaves just pop them in a cotton or muslin bag (the laundry bags for washing underwear are good for this) and hang it up shaking it daily. Always dry plant materials away from direct sunlight or they will lose their potency.

The amount of time that they need to dry will vary according to the plant and the conditions. It is always a pain to dry herbs when it is damp but if you can't avoid this try to make sure the air is circulating as much as possible and if it's really damp light a fire or put the heating on for a few hours each day.

Roots are notoriously difficult to dry because they are so wet when you dig them up. You will need to scrub them carefully to get rid of clingy soil. The stems and rootlets should then be cut off and large roots, such as Burdock or horseradish, should be sliced to speed up the drying process. Spread the roots out so they do not touch or hang them up for about 10 days. Check them daily and when they have started to shrink (roots loose about 75% of their weight in drying) they can be finished off in a cool oven if you like. You will know that your roots are ready when they are brittle.

<u>Storing dried plant materials</u>
If possible keep your herbs out of the light in a cool dark cupboard or trunk. If this is not possible at least keep them in amber bottles (old marmite jars are good for small amounts).

Section two: Water based herbal preparations

Elder Mother Tree: 'In the mist of the tree stood a kindly looking woman':
Arthur Rackham 1932

Herbal infusions

If you can make tea then you can make a herbal infusion because the process is fundamentally the same. You can substitute fresh herbs for dried and vice versa as long as you remember that the dried herb is about twice as potent as the fresh (due to the higher water content of the fresh herb) so if a recipe calls for a teaspoon of dried herb you will need two teaspoons of fresh herb to make a tea of the same strength. Many herbs and especially seeds have volatile oils that will escape in the steam so never make a medicinal herbal tea directly in a cup, as half the goodness can escape into the atmosphere.

Method for hot herbal infusion

Leaves, stems and flowers lend themselves to this method of preparation because their active principles are readily available and water-soluble. Seeds

such as fennel should be bruised to release their volatile oils before they are put in the pot.
1. Warm a china or glass teapot add a teaspoon of dried or two teaspoons of fresh herb (or combination of herbs) for each cup of tea.
2. For each teaspoon of herb add a cupful of boiling water and put on the lid.
3. Steep for ten to fifteen minutes.
4. Pour and drink sweetened with honey or sugar.

Method for a cold Infusion

It is perfectly possible and sometimes preferable to make a cold infusion but it will obviously take longer. This method will ensure that the volatile oils in the plant material will remain intact and that none of the active constituents of the plant will break down through exposure to high temperatures. The proportion of herb to water is the same, but in this case the infusion is left for six to twelve hours in a well-sealed pot.

Herbal Decoctions

Hard woody plant materials need to have a different method of preparation to ensure that the active principles actually get into the water. Roots, rhizomes, barks and some seeds have very strong cell walls. For these materials a decoction is the preferred method of water extraction.

Dried materials should be powdered or broken into small pieces - fresh materials should be cut into small pieces. Please do not use aluminium saucepans for this process as they can leech toxic metal into your beautiful brew.

Method for a decoction

1. Place one teaspoon of dried material (or a tablespoon of fresh) into a saucepan add a cup of water for each teaspoon of herb
2. Bring to the boil, cover and simmer for ten to fifteen minutes
3. Stain and drink

If you need to make a combination brew that contains both herbs and roots it is best to make both a decoction and an infusion and then mix the two components together.

Section Three: Alcohol based herbal preparations

Tinctures

There is much to be said for the use of alcohol as a solvent for plant materials. Firstly it is overwhelmingly the case that alcohol is a better solvent for plant constituents than water (a mixture of water and alcohol will dissolve almost all the ingredients of a herb) and secondly because alcohol acts as a preservative tinctures last for years without loosing any notable amount of their potency. Professionally produced tinctures made in laboratories with industrial alcohol use the specific alcohol/water ratios according to recipes found in various pharmacopoeia but for home use these details are not relevant. The alcohol used for a homemade tincture is vodka or brandy of at least 38% this is because a weaker alcohol/water ratio will not act as a satisfactory preservative.

Remember to double amount of herbs if using fresh.

Method for herbal tincture

The amounts are not set in stone so if you have less herb and want to tincture it make sure that there is at least a two of inches of vodka above the level of your plant material.

1. Place 120 grams/4oz of finely chopped or ground herb into a suitable container (Kilner jars are good)
2. Pour ½ litre/one pint of vodka over the herbs, tightly seal and label
3. Keep the container in a warm place preferably in the sunlight for at least part of the day for two weeks. Make sure to shake your tincture a couple of times a day.
4. Strain the tincture through a muslin in a sieve and squeeze out the pulp to extract all the vodka (the pulp will compost down)
5. Pour the tincture into a dark bottle that is well sealed.

Tinctures are stronger than infusions the dose is between 10 and 25 drops three times a day (see the materia medica section for the dosage for individual herbs). They can be taken internally straight or in sweetened water, for external use they can be added to a bath or compress and they can be effectively added to any of your homemade creams, oils, liniments and lotions.

Section Four: External Applications

Baths

A smashing way to absorb herbal remedies through the skin and benefit from their scent is to bathe in a full body bath with herbs added. This can be achieved by either running the hot water over the herbs in a muslin bag or by adding a pint or so of strong herbal infusion or decoction to the water. There are a number of lovely additions that you can add to the contents of you bath bag. Oatmeal is superb as are Epsom salts, Himalayan salt, Dead Sea salt, rock salt or Malvern sea salt.

Compress

An excellent way to apply herbs to the skin to speed up the healing process is to make a compress. Hot compresses are mainly used to ease muscle pain or speed wound healing. All the vulnerary herbs make good compresses, as do the stimulants and diaphoretics when appropriate.

You will need
A clean cloth made of a natural material such as linen, gauze, cotton or cotton wool
Appropriate hot herbal decoction or infusion

Method
1. Soak the cloth in the hot herbal solution
2. Place this, as hot as possible, on the affected area
3. Either change the cloth when it cools down or cover it with waxed paper or cling film and place a hot water bottle on it.

Poultices

Poultices work in much the same way as compresses but a poultice is made by applying the fresh herb to the wound instead of an herbal extract. Poultices are often used to draw things (such as splinters or pus) out of wounds (plantain is absolutely brilliant for this)

Before use the herb needs to be macerated (broken down) by some means to release its medicinal properties. There are several ways to break down the herbs: for example, pulse them in the blender, crush them with a in a mortar or simply boil them for 2-3 minutes. Dried herbs or powders can be used as poultices: just reconstitute them by adding a little hot water.

You will need
Ideally a little oil to lubricate the site of the wound so the poultice doesn't stick
Your macerated herb

Method
1. Apply a little oil to the site of the wound
2. Place the macerated herb on the skin
3. Cover herbs with a strip of gauze, a cotton ball or cosmetic cotton pad, muslin or linen to hold it in place
4. Keep the poultice warm for as long as you can (using the hot water bottle method, as above, if practical).

Liniments

A liniment is an external rub to stimulate muscles and ligaments they are generally based in alcohol or cider vinegar. Liniments are best administered after a hot herbal bath to relax the body and open the pores. The main ingredient is usually cayenne pepper. The following remedy is just great for any aching joints or muscles as well as arthritic or rheumatic pain!

A Very Good Liniment

You will need
A saucepan with a lid
A couple of bottles to store

1 tablespoon cayenne pepper
2 teaspoons golden seal
2 teaspoons myrrh powder
1 pint of apple cider vinegar
1 teaspoon of lavender oil

Method
1. Place the cayenne, golden seal, myrrh and vinegar in a saucepan.
2. Bring to the boil and simmer gently with a lid on for 10 minutes.
3. When absolutely cold add lavender oil
4. Pour unstrained contents into a bottle and use externally as needed.

Infused Oils

Infused oils are not to be confused with essential oils, which are extracted by various distillation methods. Infused oils are much simpler to make and extremely useful as they form the base for many medicinal creams, massage oils, lotions and soaps.

Oil is a matter of preference (or what you have to hand) I like either olive (not one with a strong scent though) or sunflower oil. I am lucky enough to have found a supply of pomace olive oil, which, as the very last pressing of olive oil, is scentless, relatively cheap and good for this purpose.

The following herbs make wonderful infused oils:
- Calendula
- Cayenne peppers
- Chickweed
- Comfrey
- Garlic
- Plantain
- St John's Wort (Superb bright red colour when made in sunflower oil)
- Yarrow

What's more they are a doddle to make, as you will see.

Methods for infused oils

i. Cold infusion method
You will need
A large Kilner jar or similar with a close-fitting lid
A quantity of fresh or dried herbs
Punch of either Himalayan or sea salt
Enough oil to generously cover the herbs with a couple of inches of neat oil over the top

Method
1. Finely chop your fresh herb and add it to the jar with a punch of salt (that's more than a pinch but less than a handful) to stop bacteria from growing in the oil as the herb breaks down. Or if using dried herb simply put your herbs in the jar.
2. Cover the herb with oil and an extra couple of inches

3. Put the jar on a sunny window sill for a couple of weeks shake the jar at least once a day
4. Strain, label and store.

ii. Double boiler method

If you don't have time to wait for a slow infusion the whole process can be hurried up thus:

You will need
A double boiler (see page 100)
A quantity of fresh or dried herb
A punch of Himalayan or sea salt
A storage jar

Method
1. Finely chop fresh herbs place in bowl with a punch of salt. Or if using dried herbs just pop them in the bowl
2. Cover generously with oil
3. Place in double boiler for a couple of hours making sure it doesn't boil dry
4. Remove from heat, strain, bottle, label and store

Creams and ointments
A simple ointment, which is basically plant material heated up in either solid vegetable oil or petroleum jelly and then strained is fine for medicinal use. Creams are more luxurious with such ingredients as cocoa butter, herbal infused oil with added rose water all emulsified with beeswax.

Here is a recipe for a lovely cream, which has taken a number of years to perfect.

Mama Lou's Lovely Cream Recipe
You will need
A double boiler (makeshift is fine see page 100)
A whisk or better still hand blender
Jars for storage

Ingredients
For about six 60 gram pots

440 grams any infused herb oil
22 grams cocoa butter
48 grams beeswax
1 teaspoon honey
92 grams rosewater
30 drops of essential oil (lavender is very good in comfrey, rose in calendula)
30 drops tincture of benzoin (as a preservative)

Method
1. Place infused oil, cocoa butter, beeswax and honey in the top of the double boiler
2. When the oils and wax have melted take the bowl out of the saucepan
3. Add the rosewater to the oils a few drops at a time beating well in between each addition to emulsify the mix (think mayonnaise here… same principal)
4. Finally add the essential oil and tincture of benzoin
5. Put in jars, label and store

Lotions

Homemade lotions are very nice to use they are moisturising and lighter than a cream to use. Lotions feel a little less medicinal and so they make a nice base for luxury formulas. I formulated this recipe for a base lotion some years ago and actually, I still like it very much.

Mama Lou's Recipe for a Base Lotion

You will need

A double boiler (see page 100)

A whisk or better still hand blender

Bottles for storage

Ingredients

Of course you should play with the base oils here the mixture of oils is entirely up to you so long as they add up to 100 ml all together. I invariably use base oils infused with herbs such as calendula, comfrey, elderflower, chamomile or Saint John's wort.

25 ml olive oil (non scented)
25 ml wheat germ oil
50 ml almond oil
5 grams beeswax
50 ml rose water
60 drops of the essential oils of your choice

Method
1. Place base oils and wax in a double boiler until the wax has melted
2. Remove the top of the boiler from the heat and add the rosewater to the mix a few drops at a time beating well between each addition
3. Add essential oils
4. Bottle, label and store.

Here are just a few ideas for essential oil mixes for lotions
To the above recipe add: 30 drops each of sandalwood and myrrh- for a rejuvenating lotion, or 15 drops each of sandalwood, geranium, rose and ylang-ylang- for dry skin rescue, or 15 drops each of sandalwood, rose, patchouli and vanilla- for my secret formula aphrodisiac 'Emotion Lotion'…Steady now!

The Recipes

'A good coke, is half a physycyon'
saith Dr Andrew Boord, 1536, in his Dietary of Helthe

Balm

What a wonderful plant this is not only does it have a number of uses in herbal medicine, gardening, housekeeping and magic it is also divinely refreshing in food and drinks for the summer months.

Balm Barley Water

This refreshing beverage has long been known to benefit the kidneys.

You will need

A fairly large saucepan

2 Litres/4pts of Water

½ cup raw sugar or honey

2 tbs. barley kernels

A handful of balm leaves

Juice of 4 lemons

Method

1. Place water, sugar, barley and balm in the saucepan and bring to the boil
2. Simmer for 30 minutes
3. Strain, add the lemon juice
4. Chill and serve with a sprig of lemon balm

Lemon Balm Pesto

Just stir this lovely pesto into hot cooked pasta or spread on bread or crackers.

You will need

A blender, food processer or mortar and pestle

Ingredients

4 garlic cloves

2 cups lemon balm (washed leaves)

1 cup walnuts (shelled)

1teaspoon salt

1 cup good olive oil

6 oz finely grated Parmesan cheese

Salt and freshly ground black pepper

Method

1. Place garlic cloves in the blender wiz until broken down
2. Add the balm leaves then walnuts and process until chopped but still a bit chunky
3. Keep the machine going and slowly pour in the olive oil
4. Stop blending to add cheese and seasonings
5. Blend till desired consistency is reached taste and amend seasoning if needed.

Carmelite water

This is a recipe for Carmelite water, which took its name from the Parisian Carmelite nuns who produced it in the 17th century. The water was extremely popular and was sold for hundreds of years under the name Eau de Me`lisse de Carmes and was used not only as a scent but also to treat various nervous disorders.

You will need

A mortar and pestle

2x 10-ounce sterilized glass bottles with tight-fitting stoppers

A fine sieve

An unbleached paper coffee filter

A bowl

Ingredients

2 tablespoons lemon balm leaves

1 tablespoon finely chopped lemon peel

1 sprig sweet marjoram
Half a cinnamon stick
5 whole cloves
1 teaspoon nutmeg, (grated)
1 inch piece angelica stem
1¼ cup vodka

Method
1. Crush the dry ingredients in the mortar and pestle
2. Place the wide necked bottle, add the vodka
3. Steep in a warm place for 10 days, shake daily
4. Strain the liquid through the sieve into the bowl
5. Then drip the strained liquid through the coffee filter into a freshly sterilized bottle
6. Let stand at least 2 weeks

Store in a cool, dark place.

Potpourri Verte
A lovely green potpourri can be made from a mixture in equal parts of dried balm, scented geranium leaves, lemon thyme, and bay to which some dried lemon peel and a sprinkling of orris root has been added to fix the scent.

Blackberry

Blackberries are surely one of nature's most generous gifts being both delicious and full of goodness. Any cook can turn the humble blackberry in to a multitude of delightful dishes and preserves. This unassuming fruit sits well in pies and puddings, both sweet and savoury and is the main ingredient in many a glorious pot of purple jam or jelly. Blackberries are also a welcome guest in flavoursome chutneys, relishes, sauces and vinegars. Blackberry leaves also feature in many cosmetic and household recipes and I have included some ideas along these lines.

Blackberry vinegar:
I know the idea of sweet fruit vinegar sounds a little strange but once you have tried it neat over pancakes or Yorkshire pudding (as a desert) or diluted with hot water as a comforting drink during the winter months you will never want to be without it. Blackberry vinegar is full of vitamin C and so will help combat colds and chills. Why ever this product is not available in the shops is a mystery to me.

You will need
A couple of drinks bottles with lids or corks
Blackberries (see the picture)
Cider vinegar (enough to cover the blackberries with an extra couple of inches)
Sugar (white or brown
Method
1. Wash the fruit well and drain. Cover the blackberries with the vinegar in a large bowl. Cover and stand for three or four days
2. Strain the vinegar through a sieve and squeeze the blackberries to remove all the lovely juice

3. Measure the liquid into a large pan and for every pint of infused vinegar add a pound of sugar
4. Bring the liquid to the boil and simmer for 3 or 4 minutes
5. Cool slightly and store in clean (preferably sterilized) bottles
6. Can be used straight away but in the unlikely event that you haven't used it by Christmas will keep for a whole year.

Blackberry vinegar ready to go

Bramble jelly

Blackberries make one of the most delicious jellies with a reddish-purple glow and a rounded fruity taste. The sight of a jar of it on the tea table is enough to cheer anyone in the long winter months. Brambles are low in pectin (the stuff that makes jam set) so you will need to add some lemon juice to the mix, they are also high in water content (so go easy on the water) otherwise easy peasy.

You will need

A jelly bag or butter muslin square in a sieve

A couple of jam jars

Ingredients

1kg/2lbs 4oz of blackberries (not over ripe)

150 ml /¼ pt water

1 lemon

Sugar

Method

1. Wash and pick over the blackberries
2. Place the blackberries in a pan with water and heat gently and simmer till soft (give them an occasional prod with a wooden spoon to break them up a bit.)
3. Turn the pulp into a jelly bag and drain overnight into a clean bowl (don't get impatient and squeeze or prod the bag or your jelly will go cloudy)

86

4. The next day measure the strained juice and for every 150mls/¼ Pint add half a lemon
5. For every pint of liquid add one pound of warmed sugar (you can warm it in a very low oven)
6. Return blackberry juice to the pan, add sugar and lemon juice, and stir until well dissolved.
7. Bring to the boil and boil hard until setting point is obtained (you will not get a solid hard set more the soft spreadable sort). Note: Setting point is reached when you push your finger into a spoonful of the cooled jelly on a plate and it wrinkles and doesn't immediately return to its original position
8. Skim, pot and seal

Spiced Blackberry Cordial

This is a treat during the winter months. It is used much like any fruit cordial diluted with either hot or cold water. Its spicy edge is warming and invigorating and it's good for you too.

You will need

Jelly bag or butter muslin

A couple of sterilised bottles with screw caps

Ingredients

2.5 kg/6lbs blackberries

½ inch fresh ginger

6 cloves

Stick of cinnamon

Sugar

3 dl/½ Pint Water

…And if you fancy ¼ pt of brandy

Method
1. Wash the fruits well and drain. Place them in a pan with the spices and water and bring to a simmer, crush the fruit with a wooden spoon to make the juices flow
2. Simmer for about 45 minutes until the fruit has given up its juice
3. Strain through a jelly bag or muslin into a clean container
4. Measure the juice
5. For every 3 dl/½ Pint Water add 350gr/12oz of sugar
6. Bring back to the boil
7. Cool a bit and add brandy if you are using it
8. Either freeze the syrup (defrost when needed) or Pour into sterilised bottles (2cm from the top).

Richard Mabey's Wonderful Blackberry junket

I don't know how this delicious vegan junket sets but it does every time… it is a culinary dream of purple red joy and only available during the blackberry season. It is simply divine either on its own or when accompanied by cream.

You will need
Some means of extracting the juice

Blackberries

Method
1. Remove juice from very ripest berries either with the help of a juice extractor or by pressing them through several layers of muslin.
2. Allow the thick, dark juice to stand undisturbed in a warm room. Do not stir or cool the juice, or add anything to it.
3. In a few hours it will have set to the consistency of a light junket.

A Facial Steam for oily skin

Blackberry leaves are astringent and can be used to soothe burns in an emergency

You will need
A china or glass basin

2 handfuls fresh blackberry leaves slightly torn and bruised or 2tbs of dried herb

1 handful of rose petals (or a tablespoon of dried)

Method
1. Infuse the herbs in either a glass or china basin by covering them with boiling water
2. Cover your head and the basin with a large towel
3. Allow the steam to act on your skin for about ten minutes, keeping your eyes closed
4. Splash your face with cold water after steaming to close your pores.

A strong infusion of blackberry leaves can be added to spring tonic baths. These baths, which should be taken over several days will give skin a revitalised glow and certainly improve general well being.

Burdock

The stems roots and leaves of burdock can all be eaten raw, boiled or fried, the Japanese still grow burdock commercially as a vegetable which they call gobo. Burdock roots burrow deeply in the goodness of the earth and so they are full of nutrients including iron, magnesium, chromium, calcium, potassium, protein and zinc. They are also loaded with vitamin C.

The young leaf stems can be collected from May onwards and the leaves picked during June and July. If you are intending to eat your burdock root it is fine to collect the root once the leaves have shown it is, however, always best to take the roots in the first year of this biannual plan's life cycle as after this they go seriously deep which makes them a pain to dig up and they become tough and quite bitter for eating.

The roots that you intend to make into medicine should be gathered only in the autumn, when all the energy is returning to the earth for the winter months. For medicinal use burdock root can dried, tinctured, decocted, made into vinegars or honeys and all these processes will be a valuable addition to the winter medicine chest. The dried roots can be soaked overnight and added to soups and stews during the winter.

Burdock has a number of uses in cosmetics here is a simple recipe to make a hair rinse to add gloss, reduce dandruff, encourage hair growth and make the hair more manageable: take a handful of each of rosemary (or chamomile flowers if fair haired) nettles and burdock root. Place the herbs in a saucepan with enough water to thoroughly rinse the hair. Bring all to the boil simmer for five minutes then stand till cool, strain and use as a final rinse after washing.

Kinpira Gobo

This is a traditional dish eaten by the Japanese at New Year. It tastes earthy, salty, a bit spicy, and a bit sweet.

Ingredients
12 oz gobo (burdock root)
1 medium-sized carrot
1 or 2 dried hot red peppers (optional)
1-1/4 tablespoons vegetable oil
1 tablespoon sugar
2½ tablespoons soy sauce
2 teaspoons white sesame seeds

Method
1. Scrape the burdock root with the back of a knife under cold running water and cut it into 2-inch pieces. As soon as the brown outer layer is rubbed off, the root will begin to discolor, so you have to drop it into a bowl of water as soon as possible.
2. Slice each 2" section into slender matchstick pieces. If the core of the root is very woody, don't use it. Scrape and cut the carrot the same way into a separate bowl. If the peppers are very dry, soak for a minute or so, then remove the seeds and cut into diagonal strips.
3. Heat the oil in a large pan. Add the peppers and sauté for a few seconds.
4. Drain the burdock root and add it to the pan. Sauté about 10 minutes, stirring from time to time.
5. Add the carrot and sauté 5 more minutes.
6. Add 2 tablespoons of water, cover the pan and cook for 2 or 3 minutes, until the carrot is tender.
7. Add the sugar and soy sauce and stir to mix.
8. Bring to a boil and cook over moderate heat, stirring, until the liquid has evaporated, about 5 minutes.
9. In a small skillet, toast the sesame seeds until they begin to jump. Serve the burdock/carrot mixture in bowls sprinkled with the sesame seeds

Cayenne

Mama Lou's Anti-flu preparation: (Very Spicy!)

I have often said that a shot of this flu mix feels like a shot of whisky. This similarity was confirmed and expanded upon whilst I was researching this book. I found the following in W.T. Fernie's 1905 book Meals Medicinal: 'Very remarkable success attends the use of Cayenne Pepper as a substitute for alcohol with hard drinkers, and as a valuable drug in *delirium tremens;* when full doses given repeatedly at such intervals as seem necessary will reduce the tremor, and agitation within a few hours, causing presently a calm, prolonged sleep; at the same time the skin will become warm, and will perspire naturally; the pulse will subside in quickness, whilst regaining fullness, and volume ; the kidneys also, and the bowels will act freely. For an intemperate person who really desires to wean himself from indulging in spirituous liquors, and yet feels to need some other stimulant in place thereof, at first Cayenne Pepper, given in essence, or tincture, mixed with that of bitter orange peel, will answer most effectually, the doses being reduced in strength, and frequency from day to day'.

When threatened by colds or flu take 1 teaspoon to 1 tablespoon full every half hour and hold on to your hat!

You will need

A cup boiling water
A cup cider vinegar
2 teaspoons of cayenne pepper
1½ teaspoons of salt

Method

1. Mix cayenne and salt in a bowl
2. Pour the boiling water on to the mix and allow to cool
3. Once cool add the cider vinegar

A Mixture to expel worms

Drink 1 teaspoon of cayenne in tepid water 1 hour after evening meal before bed and one hour before breakfast

Raw Chocolate with cayenne

This is the most amazing thing absolutely out of this world. No wonder the Aztecs had such spectacular art. The cayenne (as you have learnt from the herbal section) increases the blood flow and stimulates the whole circulatory system. What better way to deliver the wonders of raw chocolate?

There are only two things that can go wrong - chocolate hates too much heat so you must use a Bain Marie to melt the oils and keep them just above body temperature and should any water enter the mix it will ruin the lot. Believe me its well worth the effort....

How to construct a Bain Marie or double boiler

Here's how to make one for yourself out of a saucepan about a third full of boiling water with a bowl suspended over it and that's it... just don't let the flame lick up the side of the bowl and don't let the bowl actually touch the water in the pan.

To Make a Simple Raw Chocolate You Will Need
A Bain Marie
A Mould of some sort (a dish will do but silicone is best)

Ingredients
½ cup raw cacao powder
¼ cup food grade cocoa butter*
¼ cup coconut oil
½ cup maple syrup (or ¼ cup maple syrup and ½ cup raw honey)
A pinch of cayenne pepper to taste

Method

For this recipe once the water in the Bain Marie has boiled the whole thing can be taken off the heat

Melt cocoa butter and coconut oil in a bowl over hot water (don't keep the water on the boil as the oils melt just above body temperature and you don't want to let them get much hotter than this)

1. Sift cacao powder into a bowl
2. Pour oils on to cacao
3. Add remaining ingredients
4. Stir well and pour into molds
5. Refrigerate for about 30 minutes before eating

*Note for a harder chocolate add a higher proportion of cocoa butter to coconut oil so long as the total butter/oil remain at ½ a cup.

Chickweed

Chickweed is much overlooked both as medicine and food, it seems that it may not be glamorous enough for modern exotic tastes. However, It is our loss... for simple chickweed can be eaten raw, steamed or boiled lightly and it has a pleasant taste not dissimilar to mild spinach. Add raw chickweed to mixed salads or make it into a delicious a soup.

Chickweed soup
You will need
Glug of olive oil and knob of butter
6 spring onions (or half a cooking onion) chopped
1 large potato peeled and diced
1 carrot peeled and diced
1 stick of celery chopped
1½ litres (2½ pts) good vegetable stock
2 bunches of chickweed, trimmed and washed with tough stems removed
Seasoning to taste
3 dl (½ pt) cream

Method
1. Melt the butter and oil in a pan and add the onions, potatoes, carrot and celery
2. Turn down the heat put a lid on the pan and 'sweat' the vegetables for about 10 minutes or until soft
3. Add the stock to the saucepan bring to the boil
4. Lower the heat
5. Add chickweed and simmer for about 10 more minutes (no longer or soup will loose its flavour)
6. Blend the soup either with a hand blender or pass through a fine sieve
7. Return to the pan add the cream and reheat without boiling
8. Serve hot with crusty bread

Chickweed and watercress salad

This lovely fruity salad works well either as a first course or as a side salad to a main dish

50 g (2 oz) chickweed
50 g (2oz) watercress
500 g (1 lb) tomatoes
1 crisp apple
1 orange
A handful of black olives
4 tablespoons olive oil

2 tablespoons cider vinegar
A crushed clove of garlic
Salt and black pepper
Method
1. Chop chickweed and watercress
2. Peel and chop apple and orange
3. Chop the tomatoes
4. Stone the olives
5. Mix all together in a bowl
6. Make a dressing by placing all the remaining ingredients in a jar and shaking thoroughly
7. Dress salad and serve.

Clover

An effective cough syrup of clover and peppermint

This syrup should be taken by the spoonful as needed for the cough that accompanies asthma, bronchitis, or a cold

28g (1 oz) red clover flowers
28g (1 oz) peppermint leaves
425 ml (1 ¼ pts) water
225 g (8 oz) honey

Method

Place the herbs in a pan with the water. Cover, bring to the boil and simmer for half an hour
Strain the liquid return it to the pan and add the honey
Bring to the boil then simmer for five minutes
Cool slightly then pour into warm jars and cover tightly

For a relaxing night time bath

Make a strong infusion of 25g (1 oz) each of red clover and chamomile flowers in a pint of water. Brew for half an hour then add to the bathwater.

Coltsfoot

Coltsfoot remedy for colds and asthma

You will need
28 grams (1 oz) of coltsfoot leaves
1 litre (2 pints) of water
A ½ inch piece of concentrated liquorice from the herbalists (if available) or a couple of liquorice roots
Honey to sweeten

Method
1. Place leaves and water in a pan with the liquorice and bring to the boil.
2. Boil rapidly to reduce the liquid by half Sweeten with honey
3. Take this remedy in teacupful doses frequently

Coltsfoot compress (for facial thread veins)
Before you apply the compress clean the face with a mild cleanser. Pat some warmed milk on the face especially around the area affected by the tread veins. Allow to dry for 15 minutes. Wash the face with a soft cloth and tepid water.

To make the compress
Infuse a tablespoon of coltsfoot in a cup of milk or water. Strain the herb and place it in a muslin envelope or cotton napkin. Allow the compress to cool slightly and apply to the face for 15 to 20 minutes.

Dandelion

The young leaves of dandelion make a really delicious addition to any salad. The leaves tend to become bitter as they grow older but they can be kept sweet by blanching them (i.e. keeping them out of the light) this is easy to do if you cover the emerging leaves with flowerpots. The roots may be grated or chopped and again eaten in salad or they may be roasted and used to make a coffee substitute. Dandelion flowers are fermented to make a pleasing country wine. Dandelions contain many plant hormones and can be combined in equal parts with nettles for a most cleansing and refreshing bath.

Italian style dandelion salad (for one for lunch)

You will need

A mixing bowl and a serving bowl

Ingredients

For the salad

A large handful young dandelion leaves

¼ cup chopped spring onion

¼ cup pine nuts,

¼ cup walnuts

2 sliced radishes

Dressing

Squeeze of lemon juice

A tablespoon good olive oil

Also

A generous sprinkling of shaved Parmesan and a few croutons

Method

1. Place all salad ingredients in mixing bowl
2. Wiz up the dressing pour over salad and toss
3. Arrange in serving bowl with Parmesan shavings and croutons

I'll include this poem because remember reciting it at school

A Poem to the Dandelion

O Dandelion, yellow as gold, what do you do all day?
"I just wait here in the tall, green grass, 'till the children come to play."
O Dandelion, yellow as gold, what do you do all night?
"I wait and wait, while the cool dew falls, and my hair grows long and white.
And what do you do when your hair grows white, and the children come to play?
"They take me in their dimpled hands, and blow my hair away!

Author unknown

Elder

Elder flowers: 'Just enough... Muscat – too many 'Tom Cat' (Ruth)

Elderflower fritters

These probably sound a bit unexciting but actually they are quite irresistible as little nibbles or served as a desert... and they are so economical.

You will need

A deep fat fryer two thirds full of sunflower oil

Ingredients

4 oz flour

1 egg

5 fluid ounces water

Pinch of salt

Some heads of elderflowers (unwashed)

Method

1. Heat oil in fryer
2. Make a batter with the flour, egg, water and salt
3. Hold the flower heads by the stalks dip them in the batter and pop into hot oil
4. Remove from oil when golden brown
5. Drain on kitchen paper on a cooling rack
6. Serve sprinkled with castor sugar

Elderflower champagne

This has to be the most glorious of all the summer treats we have. If there were only one recipe I could take with me into the afterlife it would be this one. There is nothing that comes even close to this heavenly nectar especially when served chilled on a long summers afternoon. So don't let the warning about its explosive nature put you off just get on with it…you will thank me.

You will need
A little patience
A very large mixing bowl or bucket

Ingredients
4 elderflower heads (in glorious full bloom)
4.5 ltr/1 gallon cold water
1 lemon
650 gm/ 1½ pounds white sugar
2 tablespoons white wine vinegar

Method
1.	Dissolve the sugar in a little warm water and allow to cool
2.	Squeeze the juice from the lemon then cut the rind into quarters
3.	Place all the above and the elderflowers in your large mixing bowl for 4 days to steep
4.	Strain, bottle and label
5.	The fizz should arrive between 6 to 10 days sometimes it is longer and once in my 35 years of experience it failed to arrive at all, which was all very odd… but I just made another batch and that was fine.

Warning: this potion is very unstable and once or twice bottles have gone bang in my house due to too much pressure. Keep them somewhere safe I put mine in the outhouse in an old milk crate with a board on top. Just be careful.

Elderflower syrup
My family have been enjoying this simple syrup for years and I am delighted to find it is now in the shops. As always the homemade variety seem to be superior but I think this is due to the secret ingredient… LOVE

You will need
A little patience
A large bowl or bucket
A fairly large saucepan

Ingredients
10 heads of elderflower
2 lemons
½ oz citric acid

3 lbs sugar
3 pints of water

Method
1. Remove elderflowers from main stem using the prongs of a fork leaving behind very little green
2. Halve the lemons squeeze juice and put the lot including elderflowers in a large mixing bowl
3. Bring sugar and water to the boil pour it over the elder and lemon
4. Cover and leave overnight
5. Next day strain and re-boil add the citric acid and bottle.
6. It's ready to drink straight away but can be stored in a cool dark place until opened after which it should be stored in the fridge.

Elderberries

Elderberry Rob

This is my favourite recipe for elderberries and I make it every year. However much I make I can guarantee that the lot will be gone by the end of January if indeed, it lasts that long. All the family love it mixed with hot water and a dash of brandy for the adults. It is rich in vitamin C and warms the very essence of your being.

You will need
A large saucepan
A fine sieve lined with muslin or a jelly bag
Bottles for storage

Ingredients
4 pounds/2 kg elderberries off the stalks
2 × 2"cinnamon sticks
2" bashed ginger root
1 teaspoon allspice
1 teaspoon cloves
½ pint/500ml water

A couple of pounds of either sugar or honey
5 fluid oz of brandy

Method
1. Place all ingredients in a pan and bring to the boil
2. Simmer for 20 minutes
3. Strain through jelly bag or muslin lined sieve squeezing out as much juice as possible
4. Measure juice and to each pint of juice add either 1 pound/500 grams of sugar or 12 oz/750 grams of honey
5. Return all to the heat, bring back to the boil and simmer for a further 15 minutes
6. Cool and add the Brandy
7. Bottle and label

Garlic

Whole roasted heads of garlic

This way of cooking garlic is totally delicious do not be deceived by its simplicity the resulting paste is luscious, rich and sumptuous.

When making jacket potatoes I often serve roasted garlic and onions as a couple of side dishes and it's so easy: - just stick a few heads of garlic and a few small raw onions in the oven about 35-40 minutes before the potatoes are cooked.

You can also mash the roasted garlic cloves with a fork and use in any dish calling for garlic.

Garlic puree is delicious spread over warm French bread (the ultimate garlic bread) or mixed in to cooked pasta with olive oil, fresh basil and Parmesan.

Method

1. Preheat the oven to 400°F
2. Peel away the outer layers of the garlic bulb skin, leaving the skins of the individual cloves intact.
3. Using a knife, cut off 1/4 to a 1/2 inch of the top of cloves, exposing the individual cloves of garlic
4. Place the garlic heads on a baking tray
5. Drizzle a couple tsp of olive oil over each head, season with salt and pepper
6. Bake at 400°F for 35-40 minutes, or until the cloves feel soft when pressed
7. Once the garlic has cooled enough to handle… get involved… squeeze the individual cloves with your fingers either strait into your mouth or on to your plate

Vinegar of the Four Thieves (A useful protection against disease and magical attack since the 1630's)

You can take this remedy a teaspoon at a time, add it to salad dressings, use a splash in your bathwater or dilute a little in a spray bottle to help clear a space.

You will need:

A large container with a lid (Kilner jar is good)

Ingredients:

2 tbs. of garlic roughly chopped
A handful of each of lavender, sage, rosemary, thyme, rue and wormwood
Enough cider vinegar to cover the herbs

Method
1. Roughly chop all the herbs if fresh
2. Place all plant material in the jar
3. Cover with vinegar with about three fingers of vinegar over the top of the plant materials
4. Fasten tightly
5. Stand somewhere warm for about a month and shake often
6. Strain and bottle.

Four Thieves Vinegar steeping

Garlic Honey

Garlic honey... Strange combo but thinking about it... garlic's antibiotic, anti-parasitic and anti-fungal properties combined with the antiseptic qualities of honey makes this potion one for every green medicine chest. This is a great preventative tonic and it will also work as a treatment for any coughs, colds, sinus problems, cuts and grazes

Ingredients
2 whole heads of garlic (as fat and organic as possible)
450gm/1pound best organic (or Manuka x10 honey)
Method

1. Peel and crush the garlic either in a mortar and pestle or stick them in a blender/food processer and give a couple of 'pulse' whizzes.
2. Add two tablespoons of honey and either continue to pound (or wiz some more in the old blender) until the garlic is completely transparent
3. Add the remaining honey and make sure to mix well
4. Pour the garlic honey into a jar and label including the date and dosage instructions.

Dosage:
As a tonic or preventative: ½ teaspoon daily
As a remedy: ½ teaspoon 3xdaily for chronic conditions or if acute 6xdaily
Take directly or dissolved in lemon and water or with fruit vinegar
Apply directly to the skin for bites, grazes and wounds.

Ginger

Ginger is at once warming and soothing to the digestive tract where it eases indigestion and flatulence. Ginger acts as an immune enhancer and is often found in tonics to invigorate and tone the whole body. Ginger is often included in external rubs to ease aching muscles, clear toxins, relieve aching joints and improve circulation. A warm compress of a decoction of ginger root applied to the tummy can help relax menstrual cramps.

Lemon Ginger Syrup

This is a wonderful remedy for winter blues it warms the cockles of your heart! It is also an effective defence against the symptoms of colds and chills and of course where applicable the excesses of Christmas cheer especially overeating.

Take a tablespoonful (or more to taste) of the syrup in a tumbler full of hot water and add a slice of lemon and enjoy.

You will need
Sterilised bottles for storage

Ingredients
113 grams/4oz whole ginger
1 litre/2pints water
2 lemons
A Quantity of sugar

Method
1. Bruise the ginger and place in a saucepan with the water and the thinly pared rind of the lemon
2. Bring to the boil and simmer with a lid on for ¾ of an hour
3. Strain and measure and for every pint of liquid add 450 gm (1 lb) of sugar and the juice of a lemon
4. Return the lot to the pan and re-boil for ten minutes
5. Bottle, label and seal for storage.

Spicy zinger massage oil

This recipe makes a stimulating, pain relieving oil for general aches and pains it can be warmed gently before use as a massage oil or used warm as a compress. A few drops of essential oils of ginger, lavender and rosemary can be added if you have them.

Ingredients

5cm/ ½ inch chunk of fresh ginger root bashed with a rolling pin (or ¾ teaspoon of powdered ginger)
1 whole chili pepper (or ¼ teaspoon cayenne pepper)
1 cup/8 fl oz sunflower oil (or almond oil)
A tablespoon wheat germ oil

Method
1. Combine and heat the ingredients in a double-boiler for an hour and a half
2. Cover with lid and let stand an additional 2 hours
3. Strain infused oil and pour into a dark glass bottle with a tight fitting lid or stopper
4. Will last for 2-3 months in dark cool place.

Hawthorn

I do not have a great many recipes for hawthorn but the leaves make a perfectly acceptable addition to salads and the flowers can be used to make a delicious vodka based liqueur.

Hawthorn and Beetroot Salad

I've actually pinched this very simple idea from Roger Philips because it is such a good combination for a salad.

Ingredients (for two)
½ pint hawthorn leaves
2 cooked beetroot diced
French dressing

Method
1. Wash the leaves and combine with diced beetroot.
2. Add the French dressing and mix well.

Hawthorn liqueur

This liqueur captures the almond/cherry delight of the hawthorn flowers and is totally delicious.

You will need
A jam jar with a lid
Something to strain the liqueur through

Ingredients
¼ bottle of vodka (more or less)
2 tablespoons of hawthorn flowers
About 300ml sugar syrup (either made at home or from the cocktail department at the supermarket)

Method
1. Place flowers and vodka in a jam jar with a tight fitting lid
2. Stand on the windowsill for about three weeks shaking daily
3. Taste, and if you would like a stronger taste of flowers strain, add more flowers and leave for another couple of weeks.
4. Mix the infused vodka with an equal amount of sugar syrup
5. Bottle, label and store.

Lavender

Lavender and vanilla scrub for Gardener's hands

Use about a tablespoon of this heavenly scented scrub at a time. Massage it into hands paying attention to any rough areas. Rinse lightly to remove the residue then pat dry leaving softened moisturized hands. This scrub is also absolutely brilliant for dry or rough skin on knees, feet and elbows.

You will need
A large mixing bowl
Jar for storage

Ingredients
1 ½ cups Epsom salts, Himalayan salt or sea salt
1 cup Almond oil, olive oil or melted cocoanut oil
1-2 tablespoons dried lavender
1 tablespoon pure vanilla extract
25-30 drops essential oil of lavender
2 tsp runny hones
2-3 teaspoons vitamin E oil (optional)

Method
1. Mix everything together in the mixing bowl. You want a thick consistency so add more coarse ingredients if the mix is too runny or more oil/honey if the mix is too dry.
2. Place in a container with a tight fitting lid – A Kilner jar or large jam jar with a tight fitting lid is ideal
3. Store in a cool dark place, stir before use if necessary.

Marigold (calendula)

Marigolds are a useful ingredient in the kitchen where they impart a deep mysterious flavour and a rich golden colour to either savoury or sweet dishes. Their golden petals brighten up any summer salad. They can be used instead of saffron to colour rice as they have been in the past when the exotic spice was both expensive and difficult to obtain. What's more marigolds lift the spirits so you can enjoy your medicine whilst you dine… simply perfect eh?

Marigolds also have numerous uses in beauty preparations and I have included a couple of ideas for your indulgence.

A facial steam for dull or sallow skin

Make a strong infusion in a glass or china bowl using 2 tablespoons of marigold flowers, 3 tablespoons of mint leaves and 2 tablespoons of rose geranium leaves. Cover your head and the bowl with a towel and, keeping your eyes closed, allow the steam to work for about 10 minutes.

Marigold hair rinse

To Make your hair have a golden glow without using strong chemicals mix a very strong infusion of marigold flowers using a couple of ounces to a pint of water. Pour it through your hair a few times catching the liquid in a bowl and recycling it as you go.

Marigold conserve

It is said that this conserve is guaranteed to cure melancholy. It can be argued that much of its curative efficacy comes from the satisfying indulgence of making and eating such a delightful delicacy.

You will need
A mortar and pestle or similar
Small, dry, sterile jars

Ingredients
100 grams/4oz of freshly gathered marigold petals
400 grams/14 oz castor sugar
1 lemon

Method
Gather the petals on a dry day before the sun is at its zenith and use them immediately

1. Place the petals in the mortar and work to a smooth paste with the pestle adding the lemon juice as you go. The mix is ready when it has a silky smoothness.
2. Gradually beat in the sugar a little at a time until it is all absorbed by this time you should have a splendid golden conserve to behold.
3. Pot and seal

Creamy Vegetable and Marigold Soup

Ingredients

1 tablespoon sunflower oil

1oz butter

Splash of white wine or vermouth (optional)

1 medium onion

1 clove garlic

1 large potato

2 carrots

1 butternut squash

2 sticks celery

4 tablespoons marigolds

1 pt vegetable stock

1 pt milk

Salt and freshly ground black pepper

To serve

Splash of cream

A handful of croutons

Method

1. Roughly chop all the vegetables and crush the garlic
2. Heat the oil and butter in the bottom of a large saucepan add the vegetables
3. Add the marigold petals and a splash of white wine or vermouth (if using)
4. Put a lid on the pan and turn the heat to low for about 20 minutes until the vegetables are soft
5. Add the vegetable stock, bring back to the boil turn down the heat and simmer for 20 minutes
6. Wiz the lot either with a hand blender, in a big blender or in a food processer
7. Serve with a swirl of cream and a few croutons

Parsnips with marigolds and orange juice

This recipe purports to be of Elizabethan origin, however, I can find no evidence of this. The recipe is truly scrumptious though and so I have included it Elizabethan or not.

Ingredients Serves 3-4 as a side dish

1½ cups of orange juice

1 teaspoon of dried orange peel

1 Tablespoon of butter

1 tablespoon of dried marigold petals

A small pinch of cinnamon

1 teaspoon of honey

A pound of parsnips, scraped and cut into eighth of an inch discs

Beurre manie 1 tablespoon of flour blended into 1 tablespoon of butter

Garnish: Orange slices

Method

1. In a large saucepan, combine all ingredients except parsnips and *beurre manie*
2. Stir and bring to the boil
3. Add Parsnips. Cover and reduce the heat to medium.
4. Cook for 35 minutes or until parsnips are tender but firm
5. Remove parsnips with a slotted spoon
6. Bring liquid in the pot to a fast boil. Add *beurre manie* (to thicken the sauce) stirring rapidly with a wire whisk until sauce thickens. Check seasoning.
7. Replace parsnips in pot and toss to coat.
8. Place in serving dish and garnish with Orange slices.

Meadowsweet

Queen of the meadow, she was used in the past to strew the summer floors of English ladies and paupers alike. Meadowsweet has a lovely scent and I have included a recipe for a sweet-smelling bath. It is not much used in foodstuffs today, but I have found a couple of recipes that make use of her intoxicating scent and heady flavour.

Gooseberries with meadowsweet

What could be more pleasant and refreshing on a summer's day than gooseberries? This recipe has an unexpected layer underneath the tang of the fruit. It is especially good served with custard. If you want to take the recipe a step further you can measure the cooked gooseberries and mix them with half their volume of custard and half their volume of whipped cream for a superb gooseberry fool.

Ingredients

450 grams/1 pound of gooseberries
125ml/4 fl oz water (or white wine)
1 tablespoon honey (or more to taste)
2 heads of meadowsweet flowers

Method
1. Put on your favourite music to entertain yourself whilst you painstakingly top and tail the gooseberries
2. Put the water (or wine) and honey in a pan and stir to dissolve the honey bring to the boil
3. Lower the heat add the gooseberries and meadowsweet and simmer very gently for about 10 minutes be careful not to let the fruit disintegrate too much

Meadowsweet wine

This is a lovely aperitif, which seems to have some resonance with the drinking habits of merrie olde England (or merie olde England as the Victorians imagined it at least). Cheers!

Ingredients

I bottle of white wine (Sauvignon Blanc or Riesling are generally good)
3 or 4 heads of meadowsweet

Method

1. Put the meadowsweet flowers in a jug and pour over the wine
2. Leave for at least 4 hours
3. Strain and chill the wine
4. Enjoy before food

Cottage Garden Bath

A good handful of the sweetly scented meadowsweet is a wonderful herb to bathe in and especially good when mixed in equal parts with marigolds and damask rose petals for a truly pampering experience.

Nettles

Best to use the young stems and leaves, as older ones can be tough and stringy. Always be careful when collecting use rubber gloves and scissors or securers the damn things really hurt for a while if they get you. Nettle soup is a must for the springtime the first nettles appear about Saint Patrick's Day -17th March (what is it with that man and poisonous stingy things?). I have included the recipe for a fantastic feed for the garden. Nettles are also very good for the hair they say and so I have included a recipe for a nettle hair rinse.

Spring Nettle Soup

There is nothing that tastes nicer than this soup it heralds the arrival of spring in our house and so is always welcome. It's always good to add a bit of jack by the hedge if you can find it too.

Ingredients (serves 4)

15grams /½ oz butter
1 tablespoon sunflower oil
1 small onion
Clove garlic
1 carrot
1 stick celery
2 leeks
225 grams/8oz potatoes
A splash of white wine or vermouth (optional)
225 grams/8oz young nettles (washed)
3 stems of Jack by the Hedge (optional)
A handful of spinach or watercress
1.5 liters/2 ½ pints vegetable stock
A swirl of cream and crusty bread to serve

Method

1. Chop the onion, carrot, celery, leeks and potatoes and crush the garlic
2. Heat the oil and butter in a saucepan add the chopped vegetables and crushed garlic put a lid on and turn down the heat very low for about 10 minutes
3. Turn up the heat and add a splash of wine if using
4. Add the nettles, spinach/watercress and jack by the hedge if using
5. Stir, turn down the heat and replace the lid for 5 minutes
6. Add the stock bring to the boil
7. Simmer for 10-15 minutes
8. Wiz in blender
9. Serve with a swirl of cream and some crusty bread

Nettle Stinger

Enough of this 'good for you' malarkey… here's one to get the party started

Ingredients

2 parts Tanqueray gin
1 part Nettle Cordial (either buy it or see recipe below)

Method

1. Place all ingredients into a jug full of ice
2. Stir 10 times
3. Double strain into chilled martini glass
4. Garnish with lime wedge and something green

Nettle cordial

This cordial is very pleasant if a little unusual… it is great with sparkling water and a slice of lemon or of course as a component in the very boozy 'Nettle Stinger' This cordial keeps for at least a couple of months in a cool dark place
Once opened though … refrigerate!

You will need

Sterile glass bottles after 2 or 3 days

Ingredients

200 g freshly picked nettle tops
1 kg granulated sugar
40 g citric acid
500 ml boiling water

Method

1. Give your nettles a wash
2. Place sugar, water and citric acid in a saucepan stir well and bring to the boil
3. Cool the water sugar mix down to body temperature
4. Add the nettle leaves and stir well making sure the nettles are submerged
5. Leave to steep for 2-3 days
6. Strain and pour into sterilised bottles

Nettle Beer

Here's one I've made many times its not very alcoholic but really refreshing after a long hard day in the garden… try with ice and a sprig of mint

You will need
A large bucket and a very clean tea towel to cover same
Sterilised bottles

Ingredients
150 nettles
12litres/2½ gallons water
1.5 Kg/3 lbs sugar
50grams/2 oz cream of tartar
15grams/ ½ oz brewing yeast (available in brew shops)

Method
1. Boil the nettles with the water for 15 minutes
2. Strain add the sugar and the cream of tartar
3. Re-heat stirring until everything is well dissolved
4. Transfer to a bucket
5. Cool the brew until it is the same temperature as you (tepid)
6. Add the yeast, stir cover with clean cloth and leave for 4 days
7. Remove scum and without disturbing the sediment bottle in strong bottles (the ones with swing top lids are best)
8. Ready to drink in about a week

Warning: occasionally bottles may explode after bottling (the danger is largely over after a few days) so just to be on the safe side keep out of the way in a covered box before transferring to the fridge to cool for drinking.

Nettle hair rinse
To strengthen the hair and give it a shine
Take 3 tablespoons of nettles to a pint of water place all in a saucepan and bring to the boil. Turn off the heat and steep for one hour. Use as a final hair rinse.

Nettle garden feed
A very effective high nitrogen feed can be made by soaking fresh nettles in water at about the rate of 2 pounds (1 kg) of nettles to 2 gallons (10 litres) of water for about two weeks (warning! Gets very smelly). Strain this mix and dilute 1 part nettle brew to 10 parts water.

Rose hips of the Wild Rose (dog rose)

Rose hip Syrup

We would be silly Billies if we let rose hips go to waste they are an exceptional source of vitamin C and in my experience children love rose hip syrup – absolutely win win!

Ingredients
1 kg/2lbs rosehips
3 litres/4½ pints water
450 grams/1 lb sugar

Method
1. Get 3 pints of your water on to boil
2. Prepare the rosehips by roughly chopping them or mincing
3. Add the chopped hips to the boiling water and bring back to the boil
4. Turn off the heat, put a lid on the pan and leave to infuse for about half an hour
5. Pass the infusion through a jelly bag or two layers of muslin in a sieve save the juice
6. Tip the strained hips back in to the saucepan and adding the remaining 1 ½ pints of water
7. Bring to the boil and infuse (but this time for about 15 minutes)
8. Strain as before and mix the first and second strained juices together in a pan
9. Bring the juices back to the boil and simmer until there is about ¾ ltr/1 ½ pints of juice left in total
10. Add the sugar, stir to dissolve, bring back to the boil and simmer gently for about 5 minutes
11. Pour the syrup into warm sterilised bottles within 5cm/1 inch of the top seal with corks, screw tops or swing top stoppers
12. Store in the fridge

Or… if you want your syrup to last all winter without refrigeration
1. Instead of sealing tightly just rest your tops on the top of the bottles
2. Place the bottles in the deepest saucepan you have with either a false bottom or a smaller saucepan lid in the bottom
3. Fill the saucepan with water to the level of the syrup
4. Bring slowly to the boil
5. Simmer for 5 minutes to sterilize then remove from the pan
6. Dry the bottles, fasten the tops securely, label and store

And that is all there is to sterilizing syrups for storage. Easy when you know how eh?

Sage

Sage and onion Stuffing

This is my grandma's recipe for stuffing, which she absolutely loved but could not eat because of her terrible digestive problems. Poor soul. She nevertheless made this stuffing whenever the family was gathered together for a feast. I love this recipe because it reminds me of the wonderful days we spent together before adulthood got in the way and I bet my grandma is now eating it by the tray full on special occasions in heaven.

Ingredients
1 medium onion
¼ pint vegetable stock
12 oz breadcrumbs
A tablespoon sage (more or less to taste)
Salt and pepper
A few blobs of butter

Method
1. Pre heat the oven to about gas mark 6/200 C (or slip the stuffing in with other roasty things cooking in the oven)
2. Grease a baking tray with butter
3. Finely chop an onion
4. Place the chopped onion and vegetable stock in a saucepan bring to the boil simmer until onion is soft
5. Pop breadcrumbs in a dish with a tablespoon of sage and seasonings
6. Pour the onion and stock into the breadcrumbs you want it to hold together but not be too sloppy so… if it's too wet add more breadcrumbs, if too dry more liquid (hot water will do)
7. Either make stuffing balls or a slab of stuffing dotted with extra butter
8. Bake for about 20 minutes if in balls 30-35 minutes if a tray load

Wormwood

To make your own absinthe

First make a tincture by soaking a couple of large sprigs (more or less to taste) of fresh wormwood, a teaspoon of fresh lemon balm, I star anise, a small pinch of fennel seeds (crushed) in a pint of vodka for 6 weeks (shake daily).

Strain the tincture and combine it with a bottle of Pernod, Anisette, Ouzo or Ricard (my personal favourite)

And now it's time to party like its 1899...

How to drink it... it's bitter so you need sugar... Absinthe drinkers, romantics one and all, seem to have formulated their own set of rituals around the drinking of their own particular poison. The idea is that the sugar is placed on the spoon (the one in the picture is the classic bistro spoon) and cold water is poured over the sugar to dissolve it. Of course you can simply use sugar syrup or dissolve granulated sugar in the glass it's just not so ... well... theatrical…. (If you really like drama you can drench the sugar cube in absinthe and set fire to it) the ratio of water to absinthe is a matter of taste and don't over do it or you will regret it … but don't let that put you off the green fairy is actually very good company….

Appendices

Appendix i

The actions of some readily available herbs

Not all the herbs on this list are covered in the meteria medica but it is perfectly easy to get hold of any of them at any good herbalist.

<u>Alterative</u>: burdock, cleavers, nettles, red clover

<u>Analgesics</u>: meadowsweet, skullcap, St. John's Wort

<u>Anthelmintic</u>: garlic, tansy, wormwood,

<u>Anti-bilious</u>: dandelion, mugwort, vervain, wormwood

<u>Anti-catarrhal</u>: elder, eyebright, garlic, peppermint, sage, thyme, yarrow

<u>Anti-emetic</u>: lemon balm, meadowsweet

<u>Anti-inflammatory</u>: chamomile, marigold, St. John's wort

<u>Anti-microbial</u>: cayenne, garlic, marigold, peppermint, plantain, wormwood

<u>Anti-spasmodic</u>: chamomile, lime flowers, vervain

<u>Aromatic</u>: lemon balm, chamomile, cloves, dill, fennel, ginger, meadowsweet, peppermint

<u>Astringent</u>: chamomile, meadowsweet, mullein, plantain, raspberry, St John's wort, yarrow

<u>Bitter</u>: chamomile, tansy, wormwood

<u>Cardiac tonic</u>: hawthorn berries

<u>Carminative</u>: cayenne, chamomile, fennel, garlic, Ginger, peppermint

<u>Demulcent</u>: comfrey, mullein, oatmeal, slippery elm

<u>Depurative</u>: burdock, dandelion, echinacea, red clover

<u>Diaphoretic</u>: elder, garlic, ginger, lime flowers, peppermint, yarrow

<u>Diuretic</u>: burdock, cleavers, dandelion, elder, hawthorn berries, lime flowers, yarrow

<u>Emmenagogue</u>: chamomile, marigold, mugwort, peppermint, raspberry leaves, rue, St. John's wort, tansy, vervain, wormwood, yarrow.

<u>Emollient</u>: chickweed, comfrey, marigold, plantain

Expectorant: coltsfoot, comfrey, elderflower, liquorice, mullein

Febrifuge: Elderflower, marigold, peppermint, plantain, Vervain

Hepatic: cleavers, dandelion, wormwood, yarrow

Laxative: burdock, cleavers, dandelion, liquorice

Nervine: chamomile, lemon balm, lime flowers, red clover, vervain, wormwood

Pectoral: coltsfoot, comfrey, elderflowers, garlic, liquorice, mullein, vervain

Rubefacient: cayenne, garlic, ginger, horseradish

Sedative: chamomile, cowslip, hops, red clover, St. John's wort

Soporific: chamomile, cowslip, hops, lavender, lime flowers

Stimulant: cayenne, dandelion, garlic, horseradish, marigold, peppermint, wormwood, yarrow

Styptic: meadowsweet, marigold, plantain, yarrow

Tonic: Burdock, cayenne, chamomile, cleavers, comfrey, dandelion, garlic, hawthorn, lime flowers, marigold, mugwort, nettle, raspberry leaves, red clover, vervain, yarrow

Vulnerary: burdock, chickweed, cleavers, comfrey, elder, marigold, mullein, plantain, yarrow

Appendix ii

Repertory: (specifically herbs from this volume)

Abscess
Coltsfoot, echinacea, garlic

Acne
Echinacea, garlic

Adenoids
Echinacea, garlic, marigold

Angina pectoris
Hawthorn

Appetite loss
Mugwort, wormwood

Anxiety
Balm, St. John's wort

Arthritis
Meadowsweet, yarrow

Asthma
Coltsfoot

Blood pressure (high)
Garlic, hawthorn, yarrow

Blood pressure (low)
Hawthorn

Boils
Chickweed, coltsfoot, comfrey, echinacea, garlic, plantain

Bronchitis
Coltsfoot, comfrey, echinacea, garlic, plantain

Burns
Chickweed, comfrey, elder, marigold, plantain, St. John's wort

Bruises
Chickweed, comfrey, elder, marigold, St. John's wort

Catarrh
Coltsfoot, echinacea, elder, garlic, peppermint

Chilblains
Cayenne, ginger

Circulation
Cayenne, ginger

Cold
Cayenne, echinacea, elder, garlic, ginger, peppermint, yarrow

Colic
Cayenne, ginger, mugwort, peppermint, wormwood

Colitis
Comfrey, meadowsweet

Conjunctivitis
Elder, marigold

Cough
Coltsfoot, comfrey, garlic, plantain, red clover

Cramp
Cayenne, ginger

Cystitis
Burdock, coltsfoot, echinacea, nettles, plantain, yarrow

Debility
Cayenne, dandelion, ginger, mugwort, wormwood

Depression
Balm, mugwort, wormwood

Diarrhoea
Comfrey, meadowsweet, plantain

Earache
A drop of lavender oil directly in the ear

Eczema
Burdock, chickweed, comfrey, nettles, red clover

Fever
Cayenne, ginger, elderflower, peppermint, yarrow

Fibromyalgia
Cayenne, ginger, St John's wort

Flatulence
Balm, cayenne, ginger, mugwort, peppermint, wormwood

Fungus infections
Marigold

Gall bladder problems
Dandelion, marigold

Gastritis
Comfrey, meadowsweet

Gingivitis
Echinacea, garlic, red sage

Glands (swollen)
Echinacea, marigold

Glandular fever
Echinacea, garlic, wormwood

Headache
Peppermint, St John's wort, wormwood

Haemorrhoids
Cayenne (internally), chickweed, comfrey

Heartburn
Comfrey, meadowsweet, peppermint

Hayfever
Elder, garlic, peppermint

Indigestion
Balm, cayenne, ginger, mugwort, peppermint, red sage, wormwood

Infection
Cayenne, echinacea, garlic, ginger, wormwood

Influenza
Balm, cayenne, echinacea, elder, garlic, ginger, peppermint, yarrow

Itching
Chickweed, marigold, St. John's wort

Jaundice
Dandelion

Kidney stones
Dandelion, yarrow

Laryngitis
Cayenne, echinacea, red sage

Liver tonic
Burdock, dandelion, garlic

Lumbago
Cayenne

Menstruation (delayed)
Marigold, mugwort, yarrow, wormwood

Menstruation (painful)
Marigold, mugwort, peppermint, St. John's wort, raspberry leaves

Migraine
Peppermint, wormwood

Mouth ulcers
Comfrey, raspberry leaves, red sage

Nausea
Cayenne, meadowsweet, peppermint

Neuralgia
St John's wort

Ovarian pain
St. John's wort

Pregnancy (tonic)
Raspberry leaves

Pregnancy (vomiting)
Meadowsweet, peppermint

Psoriasis
Burdock, chickweed, red clover

Rheumatism
Burdock, cayenne, dandelion, elder, meadowsweet, St. John's wort, yarrow

Sciatica
St. John's wort, yarrow

Sinusitis
Elder, garlic, peppermint, yarrow

Sore throat
Blackberry, cayenne, comfrey, echinacea, garlic, ginger, hawthorn, raspberry leaves, red sage

Spots
Echinacea, garlic, lavender (oil),

Stress
Balm, lavender, St John's wort, peppermint, wormwood

Sunburn
Marigold, St. John's wort (oil)

Tension
Balm, peppermint, St. John's wort
Tonsillitis
Echinacea, garlic, red sage

Travel sickness
Ginger, peppermint
Ulcers (mouth)
See mouth ulcers
Ulcers (peptic)
Comfrey, meadowsweet
Ulcers (skin)
Chickweed, comfrey, echinacea, marigold
Varicose ulcers
Comfrey, marigold
Varicose veins
Hawthorn, St John's wort
Vomiting
Comfrey, meadowsweet, peppermint
Water retention
Dandelion, yarrow
Whooping cough
Coltsfoot, garlic, red clover
Worms
Garlic, wormwood
Wounds
Chickweed, comfrey, elder, garlic, plantain, red sage, St John's wort

Bibliography

Primary sources:

Blackwell, E., A Curious Herbal (London, 1737)
Culpepper, N., English Physician and Complete Herbal (London, 1790).
Dioscorides, De Materia Medica (first century AD) see Internet section.
Emmons, S., The Vegetable Family Physician (Boston, 1836)
Fernie, W. T., Meals Medicinal (Bristol, 1905).
Gerarde, J., The Herbal or General Historie of Plantes (London, 1597).
Henkel, A., Weeds Used in Medicine (Washington, 1917).
Hill, J., The British Herbal (London, 1756).
Lilly, W., Christian Astrology (London, 1647).
Plinny the Elder, Natural History on line see Internet section.

Books

Dincin Buchman, D., Feed Your Face (London, 1973).
Culpepper, N., Culpepper's Colour Herbal ed.Potterton, D. (London, 1983).
Cummins, P, *A Critical Edition of Le Regime Tresutile et Tresproufitable pour Conserver et Garder la Santé du Corps Humain* (Chapel Hill, 1976).
Gordon, L., A Country Herbal (Exeter, 1980).
Graves, R., Greek Myths illustrated edition (Fakenham, 1991).
Greave, M., A Modern Herbal (London, 1931, reprinted 1994).
Griffin, J., Mother Nature's Herbal (USA, 1997).
Hall, A., The Meaning of Elf and Elves in Medieval England (PhD thesis, University of Glasgow, 2004).
Hoffmann, D., The Holistic Herbal (Dorset, 1983, reprinted 1988).
Hopman, E. Evert, A Druid's Herbal (Vermont, 1995).
Kloss, J., Back to Eden (California, 1939, reprinted 1981).
Libster, M. Delmar's Integrative Herb Guide for Nurses (U.S.A., 2002)
Mabey, R., Food for free (Canterbury, 2007).
Nissim, R., Natural Healing in Gynaecology (London, 1996).
Palmer, C., Beauty for Free (London, 1981).
Parvati, J., Hygieia (New York, 1978).
Phillips, R., Wild Food (London, 1983).
Russell, M., The Complete Book of Natural Beauty (Feltham, 1985).
Urquhart, J., Living off Nature (Suffolk, 1982).
Wolfe, D. & Shazzie, Naked Chocolate (Great Yarmouth, 2010).

Internet links

Many antique and rare herbals are available to download at

http://www.botanicus.org/browse
There are many relevant classics and academic works available at
http://www.gutenberg.org/
Classics such as Pliny's Natural History are available at
http://perseus.uchicago.edu/

My Internet links are as follows

Web page: mama-lou.co.uk

Recipes: http://mamalouradford.blogspot.co.uk/

Raw recipes: http://crudaterra.blogspot.co.uk/

Hecate's herb garden: http://hecategarden.blogspot.co.uk/

Index

Abscess
  external 17, 21
Absinthe 69, 128
Achillea millefolium .... *See* Yarrow
Achilles 71
Aching joints 37, 80, 112
Alcohol
  as a solvent 78
Allium sativum .... *See* Garlic
Allspice 108
Almond oil 84, 113
Alterative 6, 13, 19, 28, 130
Amulet 43, 44, 51, 58
Anaemia 53
analgesic 11, 12, 42, 55
Angelica
  stem 88
Anglo-Norman 64
Anglo-Saxon 12, 14, 31, 34, 50, 51, 57
Anorexia Nervosa 13
Anti-bacterial 28
Antibiotic 111
Anti-catarrhal 21, 30
Anti-depressant 42
Anti-depressive 9
Anti-emetic 48, 55, 130
Anti-fungal 28, 45, 111
Anti-inflammatory . 21, 22, 28, 45, 48, 66, 130
Anti-Microbial 6, 13, 28, 34, 130
Anti-oxidant 11
Anti-parasitic 111
Antiseptic 15, 29, 34, 36, 44, 55, 63, 70, 111
Anti-spasmodic 6, 9, 19, 21, 22, 34, 42, 55, 130
Anti-tusive 6, 21
Anti-viral 28, 34
Anxiety 39, 55, 66
Aphrodisiac 38, 84
Appetite 13

Arctium lappa .... *See* Burdock
Aromatic 6, 55, 130
Artemis 68, 69
Artemisia absinthum *See* Wormwood
Artemisia vulgaris .... *See* Mugwort
Asthma 21, 34, 57, 101, 102
Astringent 6, 11, 12, 23, 39, 45, 48, 53, 57, 59, 61, 63, 66, 70, 92, 130
Athletes foot 45
Avicenna 26
Bain Marie
  how to construct 97
Bairacli Levy, Juliette De 47
Baircli Levy, Juliette De 20
Balm 9, 10, 19, 43, 86, 87, 88, 128, 130, 131, 132, 133, 134
Bath 10, 30, 33, 42, 43, 78, 79, 80, 101, 103, 119
  cottage garden 120
  spring tonic 93
Baumont, Francis 24
Beer
  Nettle 123
Bees 10
Beeswax 82, 83, 84
Beta-carotene 18
Bile 6, 25, 55, 63
Bitter ... 3, 6, 13, 26, 46, 50, 54, 68, 69, 94, 96, 103, 128, 130

Blackberry 11, 89, 90, 92, 134
  cordial, spiced 91
  Junket 92
  vinegar 11, 89
Bleeding gums 23, 59, 63
Bloating 6, 25, 50
Blood pressure
  to lower 9, 34
Blood purifier 13
Boils 13, 21, 28
Bowels 96

Bramble 11, 12, 60
Bramble jelly 90
Brandy 78, 91, 108
Breast
   engorgemet 63
Brighid 21
Bronchitis 21, 23, 34, 57, 101
Bronze Age 18
Bruising 23, 30, 31, 45, 66
Burdock 13, 14, 75, 94, 130, 131, 132, 133, 134
Burdock root 94, 95
Burns 42, 66, 92
Cacao 98
Calcium 18, 94
Calendar
   Lunar 32
Calendula 46, 83, 84, 116
Calendula officinalis .... See Marigold
Campbell, Thomas 54
Capsicum minimum .... See Cayenne
Carbuncle 17
Cardiac tonic 6, 39, 130
Carmelite water 10, 87
Carminative 6, 9, 15, 37, 42, 55, 63, 68, 130
Catarrh 30, 57
   nasal 55
   respiratory 34
Catarrhal deafness 30
Cayenne 15, 16, 44, 80, 81, 96, 97, 98, 113, 130, 131, 132, 133, 134
Chambers, John 51
Chambers, Robert 67
Chamomile 3, 84, 94, 101, 130, 131
Champagne
   Elderflower 106
Charms 10, 20, 22, 67, 69
Chickweed 17, 18, 81, 99, 131, 132, 133, 134
   and watercress salad 100
   soup 99
Chilblains 30, 31, 37

Childbirth 43, 59
   torn perineum 45
Chiron the Centaur 68, 71
Cholagogue 6, 25, 34, 45
Cholesterol
   to reduce 15, 34
Cider vinegar 80, 96, 100, 110
Cinnamon 108
   stick 88
Circe 35, 44
Circulation 37, 112
circulatory system 9, 15, 39, 97
Cleavers 130, 131
Clover 19, 20, 101
   cough syrup 101
Clover (red) 19, 132, 133, 134
Cloves 35, 36, 87, 88, 91, 108, 109, 110, 130
Cloves 88
Cocoa butter 82, 83, 98
Coconut oil 98
Cocytus
   river 56
Colds 28, 30, 34, 55, 61, 70, 89, 96, 102, 111, 112
Colic 37, 55
Colitis
   ulcerative 23, 55
Coltsfoot 20, 21, 22, 102, 131, 132, 134
   compress for facial thread veins
   102
Coltsfoot, ... 132
Comanche 29
Comfrey . 23, 24, 81, 83, 84, 130, 131, 132, 133, 134
Companion plant 10
Compress
   to construct 79
Confucius 38
Conjunctivitis 30
Conserve
   of marigolds 116

Constipation 7, 17, 61
Coughs 17, 19, 21, 22, 23, 57, 101, 111
Cowslips 10
Cramp 6, 37, 112
Crataegus oxyacantha ..*See* Hawthorn
Creams
    to make 83
Crohn's disease 55
Culpepper, Nicholas 12, 14, 16, 24, 26, 35, 38, 40, 46, 47, 56, 64, 67, 135
Cystitis 13, 21, 53, 57, 70
Dandelion 13, 25, 26, 27, 103, 104, 130, 131, 133, 134
Dandelion, ... 132, 133, 134
Dead Sea salt 79
Delirium tremens 96
Delrosa 62
Demulcent 6, 17, 21, 23, 57, 130
Depurative 6, 13, 19, 130
Devil 12, 67
Diana
    Goddess 68
Diaphoretic 6, 9, 13, 30, 34, 37, 45, 55, 70, 130
Diarrhoea 11, 23, 48, 57, 59
Digestion 6, 13, 16, 38
Dioscoides 14
Dioscorides 22, 24, 26, 38, 56, 135
Diuretic ... 6, 13, 21, 25, 27, 30, 39, 53, 57, 61, 70, 130
Dizziness 39
Double boiler 82, 83, 84, 97
Dreams
    bad 38
Druids 20, 40
Dryad 32
dysentery 11, 12, 23
Earache 42, 57
Ebers Papyrus 35
Echinacea 13, 28, 29, 44, 130, 132, 133, 134

Echinacea angustifolia. *See* Echinacea
Eczema 13, 17, 19, 53
Elder . 30, 31, 32, 33, 76, 84, 105, 106, 107, 130, 131, 132, 133, 134
Elder moon 32
Elder Mother' 32
Elder, ... 35, 130, 131, 132, 133, 134
Elderberries 30, 107
Elderberry
    Rob 107
Elderflower 55
    champagne 106
    syrup 107
Elf shot 50
Elves 32
Emetic 30
Emmenagogue 6, 45, 50, 63, 131
Emollient 6, 17, 30, 131
Epsom salts 79
Essential oil 81, 84, 113
Essential oils 84
Evelyn, John 26, 31
Evil eye
    to avert 44
Evil spirits 38
Expectorant 6, 19, 21, 22, 23, 57, 131
Eye infection 30
Eyebright 130
Facial Steam 92
    for dull or sallow skin 116
Fainting 42
Fair folk 32
Fairies 32
Fairy 40
    green 128
Febrifuge 6, 131
Fertility 19, 41, 59
Fertilizer
    smelly 24
    sweet 24
fever 9, 37, 48, 55, 64, 68, 70
Fibromyalgia 66
Fire 16, 21, 22, 51, 67, 69, 75, 128

131

First Nation Americans 20, 28, 51, 58
First World War 36
Flatulence 9, 37, 42, 55, 112
Flu 28, 30, 34, 55, 70, 74, 96
    Anti-flu preparation 96
Fluid retention 25
Flying venom 12, 57
Four Thieves
    vinegar of the 35, 110
Full moon 32
Galen 22, 56
Gall bladder
    congestion of 25
Gall-bladder 45
Garden feed
    nettle 124
Garlic 34, 35, 36, 44, 81, 87, 100, 109, 110, 111, 117, 121, 130, 131, 132, 133, 134
Gastritis 48
Gerard, John .. 9, 10, 12, 14, 16, 18, 24, 48, 56, 62, 64, 67, 135
Ginger 37, 38, 91, 108, 112, 113, 130, 131, 132, 133, 134
Gingivitis 28, 63
Glastonbury thorn 40
Glue ear 57
Golden seal 80
Goodman, wilfred 3
Gooseberries
    with meadowsweet 119
Gooseberry fool 119
Gordon, Lesley 20
Gordon, Leslie 35, 49, 135
Graves, Robert 32, 135
Grete Herball 51
Griffin, Judy 10, 135
Hades 56
Haemorrhage 53
Haemorrhoids 6, 15, 17, 57
Hag-riding 38
Hair 14, 20, 33, 54, 94, 104, 116, 121, 124

Hawthorn 39, 40, 41, 65, 114, 130, 131, 132, 134
Hay fever 30
Head 16, 35, 64, 92, 109, 116
Headache 42, 46, 55
Heart 6, 9, 15, 39, 46, 47, 49, 112
Heartburn 37, 48, 68
Hecate 26, 35, 44
Hepatic 6, 131
Herbarium of Apuleius 68
Hercules 69
Hermes 35
Herod 65
Hiatus hernia 23
Himalayan salt 79, 82
Hippocrates 14, 31, 47, 65
Hoarseness 17
Hoffmann, David 136
Homer 35
Honey 10, 31, 42, 49, 58, 69, 77, 83, 86, 98, 101, 102, 108, 111, 115, 118, 119
Hopman, E. 27, 136
Hops 10, 69, 131
Hydra 69
Hyperacidity 48
Hypericum perforatum. See St. John's wort
Hypotensive 7, 9, 34, 39, 70
Hysteria 55
I-Ching
    Oracle 71
Ida
    nymph 59
Immune system 28
In the water disease 31
Indigestion .. 9, 42, 45, 55, 63, 68, 112
Insecticide
    elder 33
Insomnia 39, 42
Iron 53, 60, 71, 94
Itching 17
Jam 89, 90, 114, 115

James Wong..................................28
Jaundice..45
    congestive................................25
Jelly....................89, 90, 91, 108, 125
Jeremiah..69
Jesus
    baby..65
Jethro Kloss.............................50, 58
Joseph of Arimathaea.....................40
Jupiter.................................9, 26, 64
Karma Sutra...................................38
Kidneys....................6, 13, 25, 86, 96
King Sargon...............................61, 62
King Solomon.................................69
Kinpira Gobo..................................95
Kloss, Jethro............................16, 136
Lacnunga..57
Laryngitis..................................15, 28
Lavender ..42, 43, 44, 64, 80, 83, 110, 113, 115, 131, 133, 134
Lavenderesses................................43
Lavendula augustafolia
    Lavendula officinalis *See* Lavender
Laxative 7, 25, 30, 61, 131
Lay of the Nine Herbs.....................57
Leech book.....................................14
Leech Book of Bald.................31, 32, 51
Lelamoure, John.............................46
Leucorrhoea...................................59
Ley of the Nine Herbs.....................54
Lightening................................20, 67
Lilly, W. 11, 12, 43, 46
Liniment
    to make......................................80
Liquorice
    root..102
Liver.............................6, 25, 26, 63
London dispensary..........................10
Lotion
    to make......................................83
Louis Pasteur.................................36
Love 18, 19, 21, 31, 38, 41, 43, 69, 70, 107, 125, 127

Low mood.......................................66
Low mood.......................................42
Lumbago..15
Lungs.................................22, 34, 65
Lyte, Henry....................................14
Macer's herbal..........................46, 64
Magnesium..............................18, 94
Malvern sea salt.............................79
Maple syrup...................................98
Marigold 45, 46, 47, 69, 116, 117, 118, 130, 131, 132, 133, 134
    soup..117
Marjoram
    sweet..88
Mars................16, 34, 35, 38, 40, 53, 68
Marseilles Vinegar..........................35
Massage oil
    pain relieving............................113
Meadowsweet..48, 49, 119, 120, 130, 131, 132, 133, 134
    with gooseberries......................119
Medea..44
Melissa officinalis.............................9
Memory..............................43, 48, 64
Menopause...............................39, 63
Menstruation...................6, 26, 46, 50
Mentha piperita ....*See* Peppermint
Mercury...43
Midsummer's Day...........................66
Minthe
    naiad..56
Monardes, Nicolás..........................29
Moon..................................18, 46, 61
Morning sickness......................37, 55
Mortar and pestle 87, 88, 111, 116
Mrs Grieve ...10, 14, 44, 54, 69, 70, 71
Mugwort 12, 50, 51, 52, 54, 130, 131, 132, 133, 135
Muscles
    aching......................................112
Myrrh...80
Nappy rash.....................................45

Natural History 14, 26, 33, 35, 62, 136
Nauen, Rafe 31
Nausea 42, 48, 55
Neo-pagan 35, 51, 52, 66
Nervine 7, 39, 50, 55, 131
Nervous exhaustion 42
Nettle 53, 54, 65, 94, 103, 121, 122, 123, 124, 130, 131
   cordial 122
     beer 123
     hair rinse 124
Neuralgia 66
New Age Travellers 33
New Moon 46
Niacin 18
Niewe herbal 14
Nutmeg 88
Oatmeal 79
Oedema 25
Oils
   infused 81
Olive oil 81, 84, 87, 99, 100, 103, 109, 115
Orris root 88
Palmer, Catherine 10
Palpitations 39
Pancreas 63
Paracelsus 9
Parasites 34
Parkinson, John 48, 64
Parmesan cheese 87
Parsnips
   with marigolds and orange juice 118
Pectoral 7, 131
Peppermint 55, 101, 130, 131, 132, 133, 134
Persephone 56
Pesto 87
Phillips, Rodger 20
Pimples 42
Pisenlit
   wee the bed 27
Plantago major .... *See* Plantain
Plantain .. 25, 57, 58, 79, 81, 130, 131, 132, 133, 134
Pliny the Elder ..14, 22, 24, 26, 33, 35, 51, 62, 69, 71, 135
Porth Killer 18
Possession
   demonic 51
Pot herb 47
Potassium 18, 25, 94
Potion
   love 41
Potions
   Love 31
Potpourri 88
Pregnancy 55, 59, 63
Primum ens Melisso 9
Protection. 20, 34, 35, 38, 51, 67, 110
Psoriasis 13, 17, 19
Psychic abilities
   to increase 27
Purgative 30
Pyorrhoea 28
Queen Mab
   of the fairies 32
Raspberry 59
Raspberry leaves 130, 134
Raw Chocolate 97
red clover 13, 101, 130, 131
Regimen sanitatis Salernitanum 43, 64
Rheumatism 13, 15, 17, 25, 30, 42, 48, 66
Riboflavin 18
Richard Mabley 92, 114
Ringworm 34
Rock salt 79
Rodger Phillips 136
Romans 3, 14, 24, 33, 35, 53, 54, 58
Rosa canina
   Dog rose .... *See* Rose hips
Rose hip 62, 125

Rose water 82, 84
Roundworms 68
Rubefacient 7, 15, 37, 42, 131
Rubus fruticosus .... See Blackberry
Russian Penicillin 36
Rutin 18
Sage ... 21, 24, 51, 63, 64, 65, 127, 130, 133, 134
   and onion stuffing 127
Saint Patrick 54, 58, 121
Salicylic acid 12, 48
Salmonella 36
Salvia officinallis .... See Sage
Sambucus nigra .... See Elder
Saturn 24
Schulze, Richard 15
Sciatica 66
Scrying 52
Second Wold War 62
Second World War 36
Sedative 7, 66, 131
Selenium 18
senses
   to highten 9
Septicaemia 28
Shakespeare, William 14
Sialagogue 7, 15
Sinuses
   blocked 28
Sinusitis 21, 30
Sinusus 111
Sioux 29
Skin disorders 13
Skin eruptions 13
Skullcap 130
Smallpox 29
Snakebites 29
Soporific 7, 131
Sore nipples 45
Sore throat 29, 59
Sores 13, 31
Soup
   chickweed 99

   marigold and creamy veg 117
   nettle 121
Spells
   wish fulfilment 31
Spiraea ulmaria ...... See Meadowsweet
Spirit
   to cheer 11
   to lift 9
Spots 42
Sprains 23, 30, 31, 37
St John's wort 65, 66, 67, 81, 130, 131, 132, 133, 134
Staphylococcus 36
Stellaria media .... See Chickweed
Stimulant 7, 15, 37, 38, 50, 96, 131
Strains 23, 45
Strewing herbs 48
Stuffing
   sage and onion 127
Styptic 7, 70, 131
Sumeria 35, 61
Summer Solstice 66
Sun 51, 66
Sunburn 66
Symphytum officinale ...... See Comfrey
Syrup
   of elderflower 107
   Rose hip 125
Tansy 64, 130
Taraxacum officinale ... See Dandelion
Tea-tree oil 45
The Knight of the Burning Pestle ... 24
Theseus 26
Thread worms 68
Throat 16, 21, 23, 39, 63, 69
   sore 12
Thyme 130
Tincture 78
Tincture of benzoin 83
Tincture of myrrh 15
Tobacco
   British 22
   Herbal 20

Tonic ... 7, 9, 11, 14, 15, 19, 25, 39, 42, 46, 50, 53, 55, 59, 61, 68, 93, 111, 131
    for hair 14
Tonsillitis 28
Tonsils 6, 63
Toothaches 29
Traditional Travellers 33
Travel sickness 37, 55, 58
Tree calendar 32
Trefoil 67
Trifolium pratense .. *See* Clover (Red)
Triple goddess 32
Tussilago farfara .... *See* Coltsfoot
Ulcers
    Peptic 48
    External 17, 21
    Gastric and Duodenal 23
    Mouth 59, 63
    Skin 45
    Stomach or duodenal 45
    Varicose 23
Ulysses 35
Urtica dioica .... *See* Nettle
Uterus 14, 46
Vampires 35
Vanilla 115
Varicose veins 66
Venus 11, 14, 19, 21, 31, 48, 50, 56, 57, 59, 70
Vervain 67, 130, 131
Virgin Mary 65
Virus 34

Vitamin C 11, 18, 53, 60, 61, 89, 94, 108, 125
Vitamins 18, 57, 60
Vodka 78, 88, 114, 128
    for tincture 78
Vulnerary 7, 17, 23, 30, 45, 66, 131
W. Lilly 135
Walton, Izack 43
Wearyall Hill 40
Wheat germ oil 84, 113
Whooping cough 19, 21, 34
Winter solstice 32
Witch 44, 46, 67
Witchcraft
    evil 20
Witches 32
Woden
    the God 12
Wolfe, David 16
Womb 46, 50, 59
Worms 35, 68, 97
Wormwood 68, 69, 110, 128, 130, 131, 132, 133, 134
Wormwood, ... 69, 128, 130, 131
Wound-healing 23
Wounds ... 7, 13, 18, 23, 24, 30, 31, 44, 67, 70, 71, 79, 111
Yarrow 25, 43, 55, 70, 71, 74, 81, 130, 131, 132, 133, 134, 135
Yellow dock 13
Zeus 59
Zinc 18, 22, 57, 94
Zingiber officinale .... *See* Ginger

Printed in Great Britain
by Amazon